The Early History of Montgomery County Kentucky

Edward P. McCullough

HERITAGE BOOKS
2008

HERITAGE BOOKS
AN IMPRINT OF HERITAGE BOOKS, INC.

Books, CDs, and more—Worldwide

For our listing of thousands of titles see our website
at
www.HeritageBooks.com

Published 2008 by
HERITAGE BOOKS, INC.
Publishing Division
100 Railroad Ave. #104
Westminster, Maryland 21157

Copyright © 2006 Edward P. McCullough

All rights reserved. No part of this book may be reproduced or transmitted in any form or by any means, electronic or mechanical, including photocopying, recording or by any information storage and retrieval system without written permission from the author, except for the inclusion of brief quotations in a review.

International Standard Book Numbers
Paperbound: 978-0-7884-4289-6
Clothbound: 978-0-7884-7673-0

This book is dedicated to the Montgomery County, Kentucky Historical Society and their efforts to preserve the county's rich heritage.

Table of Contents

The Mounds of Montgomery County	1 – 21
Indian Old Fields	22 – 35
Estill's Defeat	36 – 48
Morgan's Station	49– 76
Montgomery County and the War of Rebellion	77 – 107
Court Day	108 – 115
Notes	116 – 124
Author's Notes	125 – 135
Index	136 – 139

FOREWORD

I began to write these stories on the early history of Montgomery County, Kentucky, after reading Harry G. Enoch's excellent book, *In Search of Morgan's Station, and the Last Indian Raid in Kentucky*. It was from this book that I realized how little I knew of the rich and extensive history of the county in which I was raised. I believe that my lack of knowledge on these subjects is representative of the majority of people in my generation who were raised in Montgomery County. And so I set out to learn about the history of Montgomery County, going to many of the original sources that I noted had been cited in various historical accounts, including the extensive manuscripts collected by Lymon C. Draper, the archeological surveys conducted at various times by W. D. Funkhouser and W. S. Webb from the University of Kentucky, and interviewing several of the well-known county historians. Other sources that I have cited based their accounts on these same original sources, and I have satisfied myself as to their citings. I have strayed slightly across the borders of the county in order to present a more comprehensive view of the area.

My intent for these essays is to commit to writing a body of knowledge that has not been fully passed down from one generation to the next. For example, in twelve years of schooling in Montgomery County, we did not have a single field trip to any of the Indian mounds or battle sites, or have a discussion of the rich history of the county. The Montgomery County Historical Society is doing a marvelous job on a volunteer basis to preserve historical anecdotes, but from my point of view the body of knowledge is slowly slipping away.

By no means do I assume to claim that these essays are scholarly works, and any errors or omissions are solely my fault. I am sure that additional work and study can add volumes to these essays.

I do want to acknowledge the contributions of those who have helped me and encouraged me in the preparation of these essays. Particular thanks are extended to Harry G. Enoch, who has graciously talked with me for hours; Allen J. Prewitt, who assumed a true interest in these subjects and rounded up maps and documents for me; and John Marshall Prewitt and Judge Caswell Lane, who have provided additional legends and insights to further complete the subjects. And to George Stone, Jim Browning, the University of Kentucky Department of Anthropology, and those who have read and critiqued these essays and helped make them better I am indebted.

Edward P. McCullough
Franklin, Tennessee
2006

The Mounds of Montgomery County
And the Earliest Inhabitants of the Area

Early History

For thousands of years Indian nations had ebbed and flowed throughout the Ohio Valley region, encompassing West Virginia, western Pennsylvania, Ohio, Indiana, Illinois and Kentucky. Only the Wallam Olum – The Red Record – provides any narrative in written form by the Native North American Indians as to their history. The Wallam Olum was written by the Delaware Indians, who in their own language are called the Lenni-Lenapi. The Wallam Olum records in pictures and words the historical saga of the Lenni-Lenapi, who were also known as the Algonquians. The balance of the Native North American Indians left no written language with which to give us their history. We are only able to gather their stories through oral traditions and the evidence they left behind.

It is said in the Wallam Olum that the first great nation to inhabit the Ohio Valley region well over a thousand years ago were called the Alligewi. The Alligewi lived in the large towns east of the Mississippi River and north toward the Great Lakes. They were an industrious people and traded as far west as the Rocky Mountains and as far south as the Gulf of Mexico, and they are said to have been a very tall and stout people. They were a settled agrarian society, and enjoyed a rich, structured culture. Their towns included fortifications, and they are said to be one of the most powerful Indian nations at this time in America.[1]

The Lenni-Lenapi Indians, seeking a new land to settle, approached from the west and at the Mississippi River requested permission to pass through the lands of the Alligewi. The Alligewi granted permission. But soon they became alarmed at the number of Lenni-Lenapi who were in their lands, and the Alligewi attacked the Lenni-Lenapi. The Iroquois had been observing the attacks, and offered to ally themselves with the Lenni-Lenapi and make war against the Alligewi. Great battles were fought, and no quarter was given on either side. Over the years it became evident to the Alligewi that they could not persist and win, and finally they abandoned their rich lands and fled south and settled in the southern states from Mississippi to the Appalachian Mountains. The Lenni-Lenapi and the Iroquois divided the rich land among themselves and lived in the new country in harmony for many years. Eventually the Lenni-Lenapi continued their migration eastward to the lands of the Delaware River, which was given its name from these Indians. The Iroquois, fearing that the Alligewi would return and retaliate, moved to the lands north of the Delawares into what is now New York and Canada.[2]

The Cherokees have a tradition of having lived in the north before migrating to the Carolinas, and became embroiled in a war between the Delawares and the Iroquois and formed an alliance with the Delawares, known as the Powhatan Confederacy. Eventually the Cherokees migrated to a more peaceful area south of the warring Delawares and Iroquois.

Reverend John P. Campbell related a story of how Colonel James Moore of Kentucky had been told by an old Indian that the primitive inhabitants of the state had perished in a war of extermination waged against them by the Indians; that the last great battle was fought at the Falls of the Ohio (site of current Louisville, Kentucky); and that the Indians succeeded in driving the aborigines onto a small island where they were cut to pieces (Sand Island in the Ohio River at Louisville).[3] Similar stories are attributed to the Shawnee Chief Black Fish in a story told in 1773 to Captain Thomas Bullitt, with Black Fish adding that the Shawnee feared the ghosts of the dead in Kentucky more than their grandfathers had feared them when they were living. Kantuk-kee in the Indian language means "the river of blood."[4][a]

The Mound Builders

Similar customs and traits of the Indians who inhabited these lands for a period of time have been grouped together and characterized by modern archeologists as "cultures". One great culture that left its mark on the landscape of Montgomery County is the Adena culture, which together with the Hopewell culture are collectively known as the Mound Builders. The earthen works that they left include many mounds, fortifications, and sacred circles.

The most famous of the Adena mounds in Montgomery County was so large and so prominent that it was called Little Mountain. This landmark was dismantled in 1845 and 1846 by the city which derived its name from this mound, Mount Sterling. The mound was located at the corner of Queen Street and Locust Street. Additional earthen works left by the Adena culture in Montgomery County include:

1. A mound within the city and east of the Little Mountain site. This mound was circular, twenty feet in diameter and eight feet in height. This mound was opened in August, 1924 and would appear to be a very new mound, as two brass buttons were found near a skeleton at the bottom of the mound.
2. A small mound about a quarter of a mile northeast of the city limits of Mount Sterling, which has been somewhat reduced in size due to cultivation.
3. The Ricketts mound. A large mound on the farm of W. L. Ricketts on the Oldham Pike. This mound is about one hundred feet in diameter and twelve feet high. It has been subject to numerous excavations, and no longer exists.
4. The Spratt mound. Located on the farm of Dr. S. E. Spratt on the Oldham Pike across from the Ricketts mound. The mound is twenty-five feet in diameter and five feet high. This mound was extensively excavated by amateur diggers and in 1924 yielded nearly no artifacts.
5. The Gaitskill mound. Located one half mile north of the city limits on the Maysville Pike, the mound is of

the sugar-loaf type, one hundred feet long and forty feet wide and thirty feet high. It has been dug into at various times and yielded some of the finest artifacts in Kentucky, including several tablets of distinct design, copper bracelets, and sheets of mica.

6. The Burchett mounds. The largest of a group of three mounds on the farm of D.T. Burchett, three miles northwest of Mount Sterling on the Paris Pike. A very remarkable group of mounds in the form of a triangle with the large mound toward the northwest. The largest mound is about one hundred fifty feet in diameter and fifty feet high.

7. The smallest of the three Burchett mounds is the southern-most, and has been excavated with no record of the contents found.

8. The third of the Burchett mounds is at the southeastern corner of the triangle. In the field adjoining these mounds, a deep depression shows plainly where the earth was obtained for their construction. In addition there is an oval depression, possibly signaling the site of a sacred circle.

9. A group of three mounds on the farm of B. Stafford, one mile north of Camargo. The largest of these mounds is elliptical in shape and is a sand mound which apparently has been excavated.

10. A mound on the farm of Walker Greer, two miles south of Camargo, and a quarter mile west of the Camargo Pike. This mound is practically circular, seventy-five feet in diameter and seven feet high. It had originally been considerably larger but the sides had been cultivated for many years. This site may have at one time been associated with an Indian village.

11. A small mound on the farm of Nat Young four miles north of Mount Sterling on the Mayville Pike. This mound has been mostly destroyed by cultivation.

12. A small mound in the front yard of R. T. Judy on the Judy Pike, six and a half miles northwest of Mount Sterling and one mile west of the Maysville Pike.

13.	The larger of two mounds on the farm of Lawrence Kratzer, four miles southeast of Mount Sterling on top of a hill on the south side of Greenbriar Branch. The mound has been greatly reduced by cultivation, but still covers an area of some three hundred square feet.
14.	A small mound about one hundred yards north of number 13 is marked by a number of rocks still protruding from the surface.
15.	A large mound on the farm of J. P. Highland, four miles north of Mount Sterling and about a mile west of the Maysville Pike.
16.	The larger of two mounds on the farm of Raymond Knox, six miles south of Mount Sterling near the junction of South Branch and Lulbegrud Creek.
17.	A small mound just north of Number 16 on the same farm.
18.	A large mound three miles northwest of Judy and one-half mile northwest of Grassy Lick Creek.
19.	A mound now almost totally obliterated but formerly very large just west of the junction of Aaron's Run and Grassy Lick Creek.
20.	A large mound one mile southeast of Number 19 and across the creek from it.
21.	A mound now almost entirely destroyed on the headwaters of a small northward flowing branch of Grassy Lick Creek, four miles northwest of Mount Sterling and one mile south of the Paris Pike. According to tradition many skeletons and artifacts were found in the early 1900's in this mound.
22.	A large mound three miles southwest of Mount Sterling and one-half mile south of Prewitt Station on the C. & O. Railroad.
23.	A large mound one mile west of Hinkston Creek and one and one-half miles south of Stoops.
24.	A mound two and one-half miles northeast of Mount Sterling and one mile south of the Midland Trail (US 60) on the headwaters of Harper's Creek.

25.	A mound on the north bank of Spencer Creek, one-half mile northeast of the mouth of Greenbriar Branch.

26.	A mound on the south side of Spencer Creek, one-half mile south of Number 25 and one-half mile east of the mouth of Greenbriar Branch.

27.	Two large mounds on the north side of Slate Creek just opposite the mouth of Little Slate Creek and within a mile of the Bath County line.

28.	A large mound on the south side of Brush Creek almost opposite the mouth of Bowles Fork. [5]

29.	A mound located on the farm of Jacob Johnson on the Paris Pike past the intersection of Grassy Lick Pike. Nearby was a square entrenchment with a gate on the brow of the hill, and a spring some thirty yards off.

30.	Stepstone Creek mound. This mound was located near the bottomland of Stepstone Creek, and was about thirty feet in diameter and fifteen feet high. It has been nearly completely eroded by the action of high water from the creek.[6]

31.	Indian Fort – An Indian earthen works set in a defensive posture, located at Brush Creek near Camargo on the north edge of town.

32.	Old Fort – Located on the north side Aaron's Run Road near the farm owned by Allen J. Prewitt – This is reportedly a sacred circle site.

Research shows that the Adena culture was concentrated in a circle 300 miles in diameter, with its center at Chillicothe, Ohio. There were two main Adena population centers, one along the Scioto River (most heavily populated from Chillicothe down the Scioto River to Portsmouth at the Ohio River), and the other on the Kanawha River near Charleston, West Virginia.[7]

The Adenas were farmers, rather than hunters, raising maize, beans, artichokes, pumpkins, gourds, tobacco and other crops. So much easy food allowed time for both study and improvement which dependence on hunting would not have allowed. They were traders, importing sea shells and perhaps feathers from Florida, gold and tapacloth from Georgia, mica from North Carolina, copper from upper Michigan, lead from Iowa and Kentucky, and grizzlybear teeth from the Rockies. They traded in copper ornaments, tools and weapons, basketry, pottery, wood-working, food, tobacco, skins, furs and salt. They kept accounts with quipus or knotted strings, as did the Incas and the Hawaiians. They also shrank heads as practiced by the Jivaro Indians of Ecuador. They used the lance, the throwing-stick, the blow-gun, the bow and arrow, axes, flint swords, the drill, the fish-hook, and the hoe. They smoked tobacco in ornate pipes. [8] And they observed ritualistic burial of their dead.

In the 1930's William S. Webb and Charles E. Snow from the University of Kentucky conducted extensive excavations of twenty Adena mound sites in Kentucky. These excavations entailed the complete dismantling of each of these mounds and in a few cases their subsequent restoration. From these excavations, Webb and Snow were able to expand the number of Adena cultural characteristics from the previous 57 identified characteristics to 218 characteristics. Included in the mounds excavated were the Ricketts mound, the two Wright-Green mounds, the Gaitskill mound, and the Mt. Sterling mound. From the Ricketts mound alone a total of 39 male and female skeletons were uncovered. [9] The typical Adena male was stout and 5'6" tall, and the typical Adena female was 5'2" tall.[10]

From these extensive investigations Webb and Snow were able to expand on the previous knowledge of the Adenas to encompass the 218 characteristics in trait categories including earthwork traits (such as sacred circles), mound traits, tomb traits, house traits, cremation traits, inhumation (burial) traits, flint traits, ground stone traits (including pipes, stone balls, and stone tubes), tablet traits, bone and antler traits, shell traits, copper traits, mica traits, pottery traits, textile traits, and physical characteristics. The mounds in Montgomery County have displayed a vast array of these traits.

It was also noted that the Adenas who inhabited Montgomery County lived in small "habitation groups" of two to five families. These groups lived outside of fortified areas, and normally near a supply of water and game. The burial mounds were always built on their own village, and typically the base of the mound included a burned house.[11] Several buffalo traces passed through Montgomery County heading for the various salt licks to the north, providing a constant supply of game and easy hunting for the Adenas living along these well-worn thoroughfares.

According to Robert Silverberg, "the point of origin of Adena man with his mound-building traits cannot yet be demonstrated, but it is certain that he was the first builder of earthworks in this region, and thus could not have derived these traits from any earlier occupant of the region. The age of the earliest Adena mound, obtained from charcoal found in the Toepfner Mound in Ohio, was 2780 years, with a possible error of 410 years in either direction. The latest Adena site, according to carbon-14, was the Drake mound in Kentucky, which registered an age of 1168 years with a possible error of 150 years. These figures give a range of 800 B.C. to A.D. 900. A great concern for the welfare of the dead, marked by the construction of huge earthen tombs, was [the Adena] key trait".[12]

Silverberg additionally noted that the "Adena folk constructed their mounds over many generations, adding new burials to them and increasing their bulk; in other words the Adenas lived near their mounds and had a close relationship with them over periods that may have lasted centuries.[13]

The Alligewi

The predecessors of the Adena culture, those early Indians who were noted to be very tall and stout and built fortifications, at one time or another ranged from the Great Lakes to the Gulf of Mexico. One oral tradition gathered by James Mooney (1861 – 1921) relates the story told to him by James Wafford, of the western Cherokee, who was born in Georgia in 1806. Wafford related that his grandmother, (who was probably born in the 1750's to 1760's), told him that she had heard from the old people that long before her time a party of giants had once come to visit the Cherokee (most likely when the Cherokee lived in the Appalachian Mountains of the Carolinas and Tennessee). They were nearly twice as tall as common men, and had their eyes set slanting in their heads, so that he Cherokee called them Tsunil kalu, "the slant-eyed people," because they looked like the giant hunter Tsul kalu, the Cherokee god of hunting who dwelled in the Blue Ridge Mountains. They said that these giants lived far away in the direction in which the sun goes down. The Cherokees received them as friends, and they stayed some time, and then returned to their home in the west.[14]

One eyewitness account has been preserved in the book narrating Hernando de Soto's exploration of the southeastern part of the United States named <u>The Florida of the Inca</u>, written by Garcilaso de la Vega. In 1540 as de Soto's army was entering Alabama, they encountered the Tascaluza Indians. The chief warranted a lengthy description. "He appeared to be a giant, or rather was one, and his limbs and face were in proportion to the height of his body. His countenance was handsome, and he wore a look of severity, yet a look which well revealed his ferocity and grandeur of spirit". The conquistador Juan Coles further describes this chief, stating "When we had arrived in the province of the lord Tascaluza, he came out to us in peace. He was a mighty man who had as much bone between his foot and his knee as another very large person might have between his foot and his waist".

In 1819 John Heckwelder, a missionary who had lived among the Delaware Indians since 1772, published a book on the Indians of his region. The book records the tale of the Lenni-Lenapi Indians, and the people east of the Mississippi who inhabited many large towns. Heckwelder said these people were called the Alligewi or Tallegewi. "Many wonderful things are told of [them]," he wrote. "They are said to have been remarkably tall and stout, and there is a tradition that there were giants among them".[15]

In 1882 the Secretary of the Smithsonian (the chief executive of the institution), John Wesley Powell of Grand Canyon exploration fame, hired Cyrus Thomas. Thomas was a minister and an entomologist (insects) whose broadened interests included archeology. Powell wanted Thomas to head up the recently formed Bureau of Ethnology, specifically the Eastern Mound Division.[16] Thomas accepted the position, and gradually shifted the emphasis of the department from ethnology, or study of the current native American tribes, to archeology, the study of the ancient Indian tribes. Although limited in time, with limited budget and understaffed, Thomas began the work of excavations of Indian mounds in West Virginia, Arkansas, Mississippi, Alabama, Georgia, Florida, Tennessee, North Carolina, Kentucky, Ohio, Indiana, Illinois and Wisconsin.[17] A series of Annual Reports were issued by the Bureau of Ethnology to the Secretary of the Smithsonian covering the details of the work performed and the findings. The first report issued on the subject of the mounds was the 5th Annual Report, published in 1887. The culmination of this archeological research into the Mounds and earthworks was the mammoth 730 page 12th Annual Report of the Bureau of Ethnology to the Secretary of the Smithsonian Institution 1890-1891 that was published in 1894.

A typical passage found in the 12th Annual Report, such as the details on the excavations on the Etowah mounds in Georgia, contains the following: "Grave a, a stone sepulcher 2 1/2 feet wide, 8 feet long, and 2 feet deep, was formed by placing steatite slabs on edge at the sides and ends, and across the top. The bottom consisted simply of earth hardened by fire. It contained the remains of a single skeleton, lying on its back, with the head east. The frame was heavy and about 7 feet long. The head rested on a thin copper plated ornamented with impressed figures."

The average Adena has been shown to be approximately 5 feet 6 inches in height, and yet when a seven-foot long skeleton is discovered, the fact only brings a casual mention and no further follow-up. An extremely tall skeleton does not seem to surprise Thomas or the men actually excavating these sites.

Additional findings of giants were recorded from Illinois to West Virginia with no particular note made in the 12th Annual Report. In Pike County, Illinois, the excavation report included the following: "Excepting one, which was rather more than 7 feet long, these skeletons appeared to be of medium size and many of them much decayed". In Roane County, Tennessee it was noted "At the bottom of this, resting on the original surface of the ground, was a very large skeleton, lying horizontally at full length. The length from the base of the skull to the bones of the toes was found to be 7 feet 3 inches. It is probable, therefore, that this individual when living was fully 71/2 feet tall". In Kanawha County, West Virginia in the excavation of mound number 11, it was noted, "In the center, 3 feet below the surface, was a vault 8 feet long and 3 feet wide. In the bottom of this, among the decayed fragments of bark wrappings, lay a skeleton fully 7 feet long, extended at full length on the back, head west". In the Great Smith Mound in Kanawha County, West Virginia it was noted that "Nineteen feet from the top the bottom of the debris was reached, where, in the remains of a bark coffin, a skeleton, measuring 71/2 feet in length and 19 inches across the shoulders, was discovered".

Other sources report finding skeletons of 7 feet or more in Williamson County, Tennessee; White County, Tennessee; Ashland County, Ohio; Brewersville, Indiana; and Gasterville, Pennsylvania.

And interestingly, the vast majority of these giant skeletons found were at or near the bottom of the mounds, indicating an early burial in the life of the mound. In most cases additional burials were found above these skeletons, and most of these were of a more "normal" size. In some way it appears that these extremely tall people were venerated and some of the mounds were initiated in their ritualistic burial, followed later by burials of men, women and children. Were they chiefs, warriors, holy men, or perhaps the last of an aboriginal group who were held in high esteem by a newer occupant of the land? Perhaps these were the last of the Alligewi. Unfortunately, we may never know the full extent of the story that had been preserved in the mounds. Erosion, farming, encroachment, and wanton destruction have reduced the total number of mounds in existence today to a small fraction of the number that existed 300 years ago. In fact, nearly all the mounds that Thomas studied in his various reports to the Smithsonian have since been destroyed, except a few preserved in public parks.[18]

Excavations and Findings in Montgomery County

In Montgomery County it is remarkable the state of good preservation of Indian mounds and sites that can still be identified. In Reports in Anthropology and Archeology Volume II published in 1935, W.S. Webb and W.D. Funkhouser identified twenty-eight sights in Montgomery County, "most of which are mounds of considerable size and interest". The authors stated that "Archaeologically Montgomery County is one of the richest counties in the state. From the earliest historical times it has been famous for its mounds, among which are some of the largest and finest in Kentucky. Moreover, many of these mounds have been so well preserved that their size and contour have remained practically unchanged". It is believed that a larger than normal Adena population lived in the area for quite some time. The area also had multiple buffalo traces that provided for game, ample streams for water, and the Warrior's Trace - an Indian path that extended from the Great Lakes through the Cumberland Gap to St. Augustine, Florida – passed directly through Mount Sterling and also through the southeast corner of Montgomery County. (See the map on Trails and Indian Paths in the chapter on "Indian Old Fields"). The following is a summary of the findings from a few of these sites.

Little Mountain Mound

The Little Mountain Indian mound, from which Mount Sterling derived its name, was situated near Hinkston Creek on a buffalo trace that ran from Boonesborough to the salt licks in Bath County. The mound was situated at what is the current intersection of Queen Street and Locust Street in Mount Sterling. It was a very large, perfectly circular mound, measuring some 25 feet high and 125 feet in diameter, and was such a prominent feature that it was used as a survey point by William Calk and Enoch Smith to stake land claims in 1775. In the fall of 1845 it was resolved by the city to remove the mound, and within a year it was completely razed. There were no professional archeologists attending to the dismantling of the mound, although some care was used by the residents involved in order to preserve any artifacts recovered. During this period of time the origins and purposes of the Indian mounds was far from certain, and many theories and hypothesis were being advanced. The dirt and clay from the mound was baked into bricks and used in the construction of a nearby residence.

On July 22, 1846 the Louisville Journal newspaper published an extensive letter to the editor from Mr. E.P. Buckner reporting on the dismantling of the famous mound and the discoveries made. [19] Mr. Buckner states, "Several skeletons have been dug up at different times in a good state of preservation: the teeth, particularly, had the enamel on them apparently as perfect as ever. They were buried without any uniformity; some with their heads toward the north, some toward the south, and some sitting up. These were thought to be considerable discoveries, and indeed they are, for they prove incontestably that the mound is of artificial origin". Toward the center of the mound, two skeletons of particular interest were found. "The dirt was then carefully taken away from one, and there was found about its neck a great number of small sea or lake shells about the size of a periwinkle, with the sharp end ground off so as to string them from the neck. The most superficial examination of them will convince any intelligent man that they have their origin in the sea or lakes. After the removal of this one, the other was carefully exhumed and a like quantity of beads was found about its neck and breast, but of an entirely different kind. They are round, with a hole through them, and are made of a solid ivory-like kind of bone, with a very fine polish. The number found shows that the same neck wore several strands. But upon the breast of the same skeleton was found a breastplate of copper, with a beautiful piece of apparent marble, neatly worked to fit upon it quite mechanically. It is an oblong square, scalloped on the sides and ends and rounded on the corners, weighing seven ounces and a half, precisely. It is six inches and a half long and four inches and three-eighths in width at each end. There are two holes in the middle of it about an inch and a half apart. The piece of stone weighs seven ounces and a quarter. It is five inches and a half in length, one and an eighth in width at each end, and two in the middle. It has two holes through it corresponding to those upon the breastplate, and fits down upon it with a flat side, the upper part being oval. By the side of the same frame, there were a number of flint arrow points of the finest size, make, and color I ever saw. The two skeletons, with all the above-named things, were twenty feet under ground, and measuring from them in any other direction, than in a perpendicular line to the top of the mound, they are farther than this from the surface".

    In this same report other skeletons were noted to have been found with copper bracelets around each wrist bone weighing nearly two ounces each and represent copper wire that had been bent to fit the wearer. In addition some scattered pottery of red clay was discovered, about a quart of ivory beads and copper beads all fashioned to look alike, additional broken stone breast plates, a tube three to four inches long made of stone (resembling that much of a mouth of a shotgun), a number of bones buried in an orderly fashion that seem to be used for sticking purposes, along with some kind of blue looking rock. Also noted in the mound were several thick strata of ash and coal, some 5 to 6 inches thick and seven to eight feet in area. The excavation work was estimated to haul away nearly one hundred thousand cartloads of dirt and clay, leaving Mr. Buckner to ponder how the Indians actually constructed the mound, and over what period of time. The conclusion drawn was that this mound, certainly whose purpose was for burial, was of "high antiquity".

The Ricketts Mound
The Ricketts Mound site was subject to many excavations, some amateur and some completed by W.D. Funkhouser and W.S. Webb of the University of Kentucky. In the summer of 1934 Funkhouser and Webb, armed with a grant under the Federal Emergency Relief Administration (more commonly known as the Work Relief Program) that supplied 60 men as laborers for the complete dismantling of the mound site, commenced a thorough excavation. Picks and shovels were provided by Mayor W. R. McKee of Mt. Sterling. Previous excavations included one extensive dig in about 1915 by George B. Cockrell, who at the time owned the land, and several skeletons were unearthed with a considerable number of artifacts. Later his nephew Mr. Clell Cockrell made an excavation on the west side of the mound. In 1924 Funkhouser dug several trenches in the mound but nothing significant was found.[20]

The 1934 excavation by Funkhouser and Webb, "was as thorough as could be made under the circumstances", but did not include that portion of the mound (near the center) where previous excavations had disturbed the site. In 1937 the statewide Works Progress Administration Archeological Project made it possible to excavate completely several mounds in the region, and Webb was particularly anxious to examine that portion of the Ricketts mound not studied in 1934. In April, 1940 Webb issued a much more thorough report in Reports in Anthropology and Archaeology, Volume III, Number 6: Ricketts Site Revisited.

The Ricketts Mound is located about four and a half miles south of Mount Sterling on the Oldham Pike, halfway down a sloping hill at the foot of which is a small stream. The Mound is nearly circular, about 100 feet in diameter and 12 feet high. The Mound is composed of earth and large rocks. The earth is probably from the surface of the neighboring fields, and the large, heavy sandstone rocks from the neighboring creek bed. A few of the rock piles were of considerable size and had apparently been arranged in a definite way, although it was noted that the rocks did not actually mark a burial site as had been supposed. Scattered throughout the floor of the mound were fire pits, some of considerable size, which showed evidence of much use. They were characterized by the presence of ashes, charcoal and burned and charred animal bones. Those [fire pits], which were on the floor of the mound, had burned the clay as hard as brick. The skeletal remains found throughout the mound were for the most part in very poor and fragile condition, with considerable fracture of the skulls and bones.[21]

  The site is of definite Adena culture. In the <u>Ricketts Site Revisited</u> the total tabulation for both the 1934 and the 1937 excavations was 43 burials. The site had several items of note, both for what was found, and what was not found. No old adults over the age of 56 were found buried in the mound. Only two women and three children were found buried in the mound. The average height of the adult males was approximately five feet six inches. There were seven double burials, one with a female and a male in a manner, which implied a posture of embrace between the two figures, and another with a female and a child. Five burials by cremation were noted near the Mound floor. Seven burials were in rectangular log tombs. Artifacts of bone, antler and shell were found, but only 10 projectile points (arrowheads) were found. A few copper rings, beads and bracelets were found. One stone elbow pipe showing evidence of extensive use was recovered. More interestingly, not a single piece of pottery was found in the mound.

Most Adena mounds were built upon or very near to a village or dwelling, and include pottery vessels with the burials. This leads the authors to debate whether or not this was a remote burial site of some kind, or that the evidence of the village has eroded over time. The site was generally poor in the yield of artifacts as compared to other Adena mounds.

The Wright-Green Mounds

These two Adena mounds, constructed in proximity of each other, are located on the south side of Paris Pike near the intersection of Maysville Road, north of the Gaitskill Mound. These sites were excavated by Webb as he continued to gather data to formulate a much broader base of Adena traits in Kentucky. These mounds fall much more into the "norm" of the Adena culture than what was discerned from the Ricketts Mound.

Both of these mounds were found to be built on their own villages, and were located near a large earthwork. The first mound was built over three circular dwellings and included 13 horizontal log tombs, but no cremations were noted. There were 5 important central graves to the mound. Also found was one decapitated skull whose origin is not known, but is speculated to possibly being a trophy skull. A wide assortment of artifacts were also uncovered, including 167 projectile points, 19 blades, 10 drills, 1 tablet with a bird engraving, 1 elbow pipe, 26 copper bracelets, 1 copper ring, and 3,472 pottery fragments.[22]

The second mound was smaller than the first, and contained a single log tomb burial and one cremation that was uncovered with 6 artifacts. The mound was built over a single, circular dwelling. Included in the artifacts recovered were 23 projectile points, 10 flint blades, 3 rectangular tablets, and 215 pottery fragments.

The Gaitskill Mound

Of all the artifacts found in Montgomery County, the engraved tablets found in the Gaitskill mound are perhaps the most important of all the findings. The smaller of these tablets is 92.5 mm long, 80 mm broad and 16 mm thick and is made of a very fine-grained sandstone. The edges have been carefully worked and squared and the faces brought to flat surfaces by grinding and polishing. Only one face is engraved. The engraving has been done by cutting away the background causing the figure to stand out in high relief. Several explanations for what the tablet represents have been put forth, including: 1) The design may represent a conventionalized human face in which the circular eyes, a nose and a row of three triangular teeth may be easily distinguished; 2) If the tablet is inverted from the first position, the human face is still apparent with the same eyes and nose as before, but now with a conventionalized mouth made of six almost square blocks of equal size very suggestive of the mouth, jaws and teeth. The upper portion of the figure suggests the antlers of a deer. Antlered headdress have been noted in other ceremonial Indian masks; 3) The conventionalized human hand is suggested by the five lobes in the lower part of the figure, containing the hand with a circle on the back found in other Adena mounds; and 4) It is further suggested that the design may be an attempt to represent the head of the "winged" or "feathered serpent" so frequently found in the pottery in the south.

    The second and larger of the two tablets is 112 mm long, 75 mm wide and 14 mm thick. This tablet is made of very fine-grained clay, worked to flat faces and nearly true edges, and is almost rectangular in form. The clay has been dried and is very compact, but shows no evidence of having been burned. As a result it is very brittle and has cracked badly since removal from the mound. The engraving has been done by cutting out the background, leaving the figure in relief. The surface has the appearance of having been painted or stained, as the color is only a very thin film which on a few portions of the design has flaked off, revealing the gray clay underneath. It is thought that the tablet may have been used to reproduce many impressions, each an exact duplicate of the others. The design is unique in that it has an

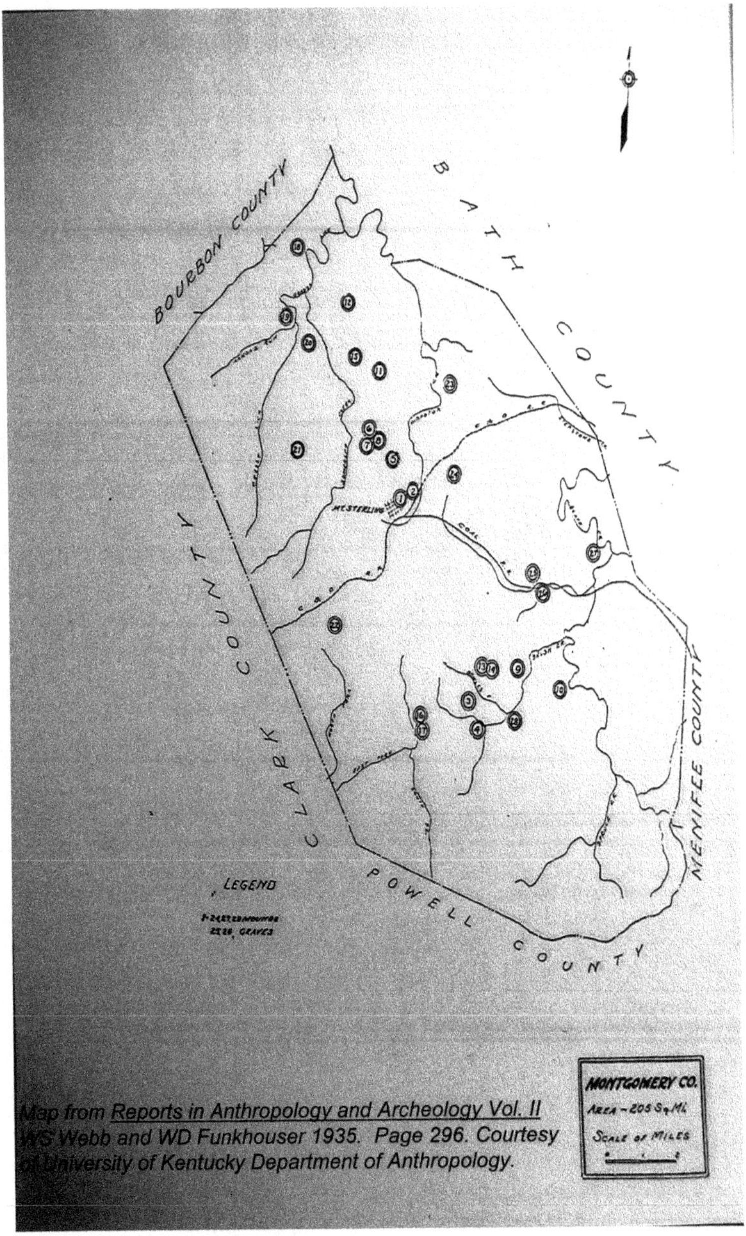

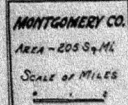

Map from *Reports in Anthropology and Archeology Vol. II* WS Webb and WD Funkhouser 1935. Page 296. Courtesy of University of Kentucky Department of Anthropology.

Site of the Little Mountain Indian Mound at the intersection of Locust and Queen Streets, in front of the church pictured above. Hinkston Creek runs to the right and behind the church.

Burchett Mound

Rickett's Mound

All pictures courtesy University of Kentucky Department of Anthropology.

Wright Mound in natural state

Excavation by WPA workers of the Rickett's Mound

Burchett Mound

Rickett's Mound

All pictures courtesy University of Kentucky Department of Anthropology.

Wright Mound in natural state

Excavation by WPA workers of the Rickett's Mound

Gaitskill Mound

Gaitskill Tablet of human face.

Gaitskill tablet inverted showing antler headress.

Pictures courtesy of the University of Kentucky Department of Anthropology.

Second tablet from the Gaitskill mound is divided into four quadrants. The tablet shows evidence of paint stains.

Tablet discovered in one of the Wright Mounds in 1937 on the property of Elizabeth Lee Wright

The owners of the Green mound have not allowed excavation of this mound, so the appearance has not been altered over time. There is a new subdivision within 100 yards of the mound.

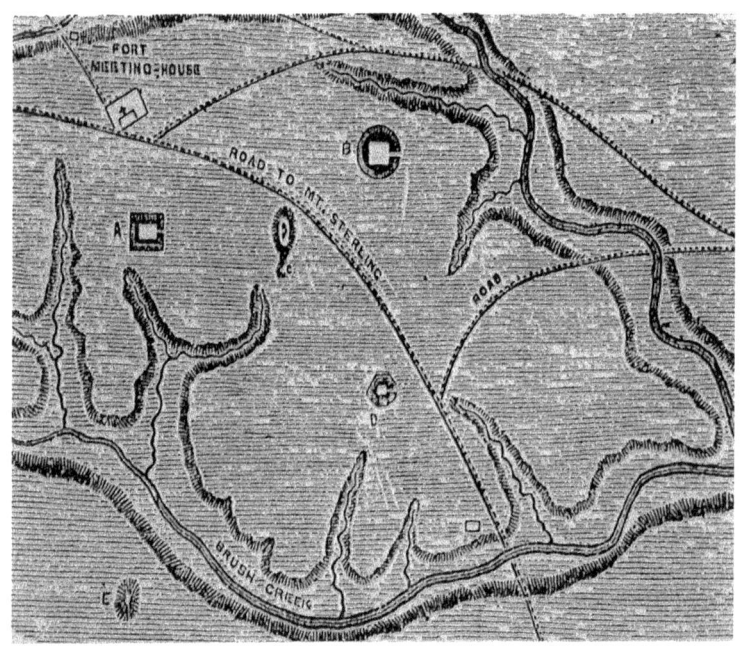

Indian Fort at Brush Creek from Lewis Collins' Historical Sketches of Kentucky (1847)

Above: Camargo Circular Earth Works prior to excavations by the University of Kentucky in the 1930s. Below Left: The Camargo Mound. Below Right: The Camargo Rectangular Earth Works. Pictures courtesy of the University of Kentucky Department of Anthropology.

Probable site of earthwork "A" as seen in 2006. The Old Fort Church would have been located a few hundred yards to the right of the trees in the picture above. The indentation in the ground at this site has the same dimensions noted by Rafinesque for earthwork "A".

North-northeast view from McCormick Road toward site of earthwork "B".

View to the east from earthwork "A" toward location of mound group noted by Prof. Rafinesque

View to the south from earthwork "A" toward the location of the large elliptical mound "C"

upper border and a lower border, and the main body is divided into four quadrants of nearly equal size. The entire design, including the border, is bilaterally symmetrical. Two possible suggestions as to the significance of the tablet have been given: 1) Each upper quadrant represents a human hand with a circle on the back, and the lower quadrants represent the human face. Since the design is cut into quadrants by the cross, this may have cosmic significance; and 2) By ignoring the quadrants and regarding the thin vertical central band as a highly conventionalized human body. The hand symbols then become the arms of the figure with the shoulders, elbows and wrist joints indicated by circles. The symbols on the lower half of the tablet then become highly conventionalized legs with the hips, knees and ankles represented by circles and the toes by five flowing bands.

These tablets suggest association with the materials found in the Moundsville, Alabama excavations.[23]

The Indian Fort at Brush Creek

In Volume II of his History of Kentucky published in 1874, Lewis Collins noted an ancient work at Brush Creek that had been visited in 1820 by Professor C.S. Rafinesque. This site is located on the edge of Camargo on the G. Greenway property. The Methodist Church in Camargo used to be located about a mile from its current location and was called Old Fort Church.[24]

According to Collins, the site consisted of 5 distinct earthworks on a broad elevated plain, 4 of which were located on the north side of Brush Creek, and one on the south side. Three of the earthworks were clearly entrenchments, and two were elliptical mounds. Describing these works from west to east:

Located on the north side of Brush creek, a rectangular earthwork was 100 feet square, composed of a slight embankment with an interior ditch. There was an entrance from the east.

Directly south of the rectangular earthwork on the opposite side of Brush Creek stood a large elliptical mound.

About 200 yards east of the rectangular earthwork on the north side of Brush Creek stood the second elliptical mound. This mound was 9 feet high and 270 feet in circumference, truncated, and surmounted by a smaller conical mound. A second smaller mound was connected with it.

To the northeast of the second mound stood a circular earthwork, 510 feet in circumference, with a ditch interior to the wall, and a gateway opening to the east. The unexcavated ground in the interior was square in form [unique to any similar works of this type found in Ohio].

To the southeast of the second mound, and due south of the earthwork noted above, was a hexagonal enclosure; whole circumference 300 feet, each side 50 feet, with a gate-way at the eastern corner. [b]

Sacred Circles

A lesser-known type of Adena earthwork also reported in Montgomery County is the sacred circle. The term was adopted from the belief that the minor earthworks were not designed to be defensive in nature, since the ditch is found to the interior of the embankment – contrary to good military engineering. Usually these enclosures are circular in form, although they may occasionally be square, rectangular or elliptical. The term has been adopted, not because their purpose is certainly known, but because it is descriptive of their construction and occurrence. They are more frequently found in groups, although occasionally they are found isolated. They normally have a diameter of two hundred fifty to three hundred feet, and invariably have the ditch interior to the wall. They always have a single gateway, usually opening toward the east. The sacred circles enclosed a circular structure surrounded by posts.

These sacred circles may have been the meeting place of a certain social set of the tribe, and the enclosed stockade-like circular structure may have been built to obtain privacy, and prevent outsiders from observing proceedings or ceremonies. Whatever their purpose, there seems to be no suggestion that the earthworks had any military value. [25]

Indian Old Fields

Located across the Montgomery County line between Howard's Creek and Lulbegrud Creek into what is now Clark County is a particular area called Indian Old Fields that included the site of an Indian village and trading post known by the Shawnee name of Eskippakithiki, which means "place of blue licks" referring to the salt deposits on Lulbegrud Creek. The Warrior's Trace passes directly by this site. The Warrior's Trace is what makes Indian Old Fields significant to Montgomery County. From Indian Old Fields heading north the trace splits into two paths, the first following Brush Creek passing through Camargo, and the second passing through Mount Sterling and following Hinkston Creek. Heading south from Indian Old Field the Warrior's Trace splits again with one path leading down through the Cumberland Gap, and the other toward the valleys of the Red River. As late as 1907 portions of this old path were still plainly discernible in places and could be followed with great accuracy for a distance. The Warrior's Trace has been called the first road in Kentucky.[1]

The Indian Old Fields area has never been subjected to a complete and thorough archeological investigation. With the encroachment of the Mountain Parkway that was constructed nearly on top of the area where the pioneers saw the remains of an Indian village, and the current construction of subdivisions and light industrial manufacturing in the immediate area, soon very little evidence will remain of what was once Indian Old Fields.

Some records from the early explorers and settlers in the immediate area of Indian Old Fields from the 1760s to the 1840s have been saved, and serve as a point of reference for what the pioneers saw when they first arrived at the site. In 1932, Lucien Beckner published an argument that the site was actually the village of Chisca to which the

Spanish explorer Hernando De Soto arrived in 1540. Beckner also argues that in about 1745 Peter Chartier led a band of renegade Shawnees from the Pennsylvania area to this site and camped there for more than one year. And in 1986 the University of Kentucky undertook a short survey of the area and published their results, but budgetary restraints prevented further detailed studies.

The Early English Explorers

In 1744 John Findley received from Pennsylvania a license as an Indian trader, which involved trading guns, cloths, trinkets and toys to the Indians for skins and furs, which were then sold in the seaboard markets to foreign shippers. By 1752 Findley was trading with the Indians in Pickawillany, near the present town of Piqua, Ohio. In the fall of 1752 Findley was bringing a stock of goods down the Ohio River where, at the mouth of Big Bone Creek, he met a party of Shawnees returning from a hunt in Illinois, and they invited him to go with them to their home at Eskippakithiki with promises of a rich harvest of furs by spring. There he built a cabin and surrounded it with a stockade so that he might protect his horses and stock. In January, 1753 a band of French Praying Indians passed by on the Warrior's Path on a mission to attack the Cherokees. Days later they came across the camp of some Pennsylvania traders, and after an altercation, took them prisoner. Feeling that they had already started trouble, the Indians decided to complete the job and on the way back to their settlements attacked Findley's cabin. Three of Findley's men were killed, and Findley and one other man made their escape, leaving all their goods and furs behind. (Unfortunately, no written documents or letters by Findley survive that give a contemporary account of Eskippakithiki during his time trading there). By June Findley was back with a new stock of goods trading with the Indians. In 1755 Findley joined Braddock's Army to fight the French and Indians, where he met a wagon driver named Daniel Boone. In 1768 Findley and Boone met again, and on May 1, 1769 they set out together to explore

Kentucky. In the mountains Findley fell ill, and Daniel Boone proceeded alone armed with landmarks provided by Findley, and on June 7, 1769 from the top of Pilot's Knob he viewed for the first time the plain of Kentucky – overlooking Indian Old Fields and Eskippakithiki. Returning to Findley, they proceeded together and made a permanent camp on Lulbegrud Creek. Upon arrival, they found the village had been burned to the ground. Filson reports Findley saying, "we found everywhere abundance of wild beasts of every sort, through the vast forest. The buffalo were more frequent than I have seen cattle in the settlements, browsing on the leaves of the cane, or cropping the herbage on those extensive plains".[2][a] Findley and Boone camped on the Lulbegrud Creek all winter and in to early Spring when Indians drove them back to their settlements.

The First Settlers at Indian Old Fields

Indian Old Fields covered about 3,500 acres of level, prairie-like land between Lulbegrud Creek and Howard's Creek. Eskippakithiki may have been the most recent Indian settlement in the area known as Indian Old Fields, and this settlement may have been short-lived. Near the falls of Combs Creek is an Indian mound, and reportedly not far from its base stood a log stockade built in a circle measuring nearly 200 yards in diameter. This was the main trading place, and is located close to Upper Howard's Creek. Previously the Indians had burned the trees on the open plain so grass could grow and attract game. The Indians grew corn, tobacco, potatoes, beans, pumpkins and sunflowers. As late as 1922 the charred remains of the palisades still provided evidence that the village had been burned down.

Among those who made early land claims at Indian Old Fields were Captain Benjamin Combs and his brothers, Cuthbert and Joseph; General Marquis Calmes, and Ben Berry. They surveyed their land claims in 1775, and when the first court was held at Boonesborough, they were given certificates of preemption or settlement to their land. [3][b]

Indian Old Fields

Subsequent documentation of the Indian Old Fields site was recorded in land dispute depositions in 1794, and the much later interviews in the 1840's by Reverend John D. Shane with the remaining pioneer survivors. All of this is "after the fact", and only reveals what they saw, or what they heard from others, when the arrived in the 1770's and 1780's. Kentucky's initial land surveys were notoriously poor efforts, and resulted in many disputes over boundary locations. To resolve the location of the property lines, depositions were given by the surveyor and others with knowledge of the landmarks used to mark the property. On March 3, 1796 in a boundary dispute involving Cuthbert Combs, depositions were taken from William Calk, John Harper, Nicholas Anderson and David Frazer regarding Combs' land at Indian Old Fields. William Calk's deposition stated that in 1779 "Enoch Smith, Robert Whitledg, Marquis Calmes Sr, Marquis Calmes Jr, Benjamin Berry, Benjamin Combs, together with myself agreed to improve this land round about this place ... and Cuthbert Combs with others agreed to give me fifty shillings to relinquish my claim to this place to which I agreed". John Harper's deposition referred to an Indian town at Beasley's cabin. "... that in the year 1782 or 1783 I know this to be called Beasley's cabin and further the deponent sayth that when ever he came to this cabin he supposed it to be a part of the old Indian Town on the place so called ..." Nicholas Anderson's deposition stated, " ... in May, 1779 I was with William Calk and others and marked a tree for Jeremiah Storkes. Calk informed me that it was not worth while for it was in the Combs' or Calmes' land. And on the same route we came to this cabin which Mr. Calk told me was Beasley's, and further the deponent saith that when he came to Beasley's cabin he supposed it to be on the land which was called the old Indian Town and further the deponent sayth that he never has known it called by any other name but Beasley's cabin ..." The deposition of David Frazer stated " ... that I have seen ... works done by Indians and other humans, and further the deponent saith that he does not know but what these works was called the old Indian Town as where I believe is two posts now stands in Marquis Calmes Junior's survey as I suppose, and further the deponent sayth that there is in this survey of Cuthbert Combs an appearance of a fort which is now to be seen". In a separate deposition in 1825, Frazer stated further that "in 1794 he saw the appearances of an old town where the dirt had been thrown up for their buildings in two rows or lines of buildings fifty or sixty yards long with a street about twenty or thirty feet between, which place the deponent showed to the surveyor this day. There was also, in 1794, an old post standing there with a strip of iron on it". [4]

Reverend Shane interviewed William Risk, who lived about 2.5 miles from Kiddville on Stone Quarry Road. Risk had moved to the Indian Old Fields area in August, 1793. "He [Calmes] put one Marchant on the place. Marchant put the cabin there about 200 to 250 yards from Howard's Upper Creek. The gateposts were nigh to it. I was at the raising of the cabin that Marchant put up by the gate posts. I heard one of the partners, General Calmes, say the old fields were all covered in blue grass when he first saw it. And when I first saw it, it was very high with grass, as high, some, as a horse's back with a head to it". Risk goes on to say, "Now on Leonard Beal's land, joining Mr. Gough's, down on Howard's Creek, the cabin was hardly a half mile from the gate posts. The point was on this side of Howard's Creek – east side. Logs in the cabin (north of Indian Old Fields) were very old when I saw it; about five feet high. The posts were two of black locust, about as far apart as a gate would be from four to four and a half feet. Were hewed. I saw the gate posts standing there. The gate posts and cabin were old ... There was a sign of corn still there, it was down by Lulbegrud as if the fence had all rotted down, and the place was overgrown with weeds. Enoch Smith was of the same opinion – corn, I think. On a branch of Combs' Creek where I made sugar one year, I found the old tap where sugar had been made, and the old tap was closed over to

ABOVE: *Eskippakithiki Road marker.*

RIGHT: *View looking northeast*

BELOW: *View looking southeast towards Pilot's Knob.*

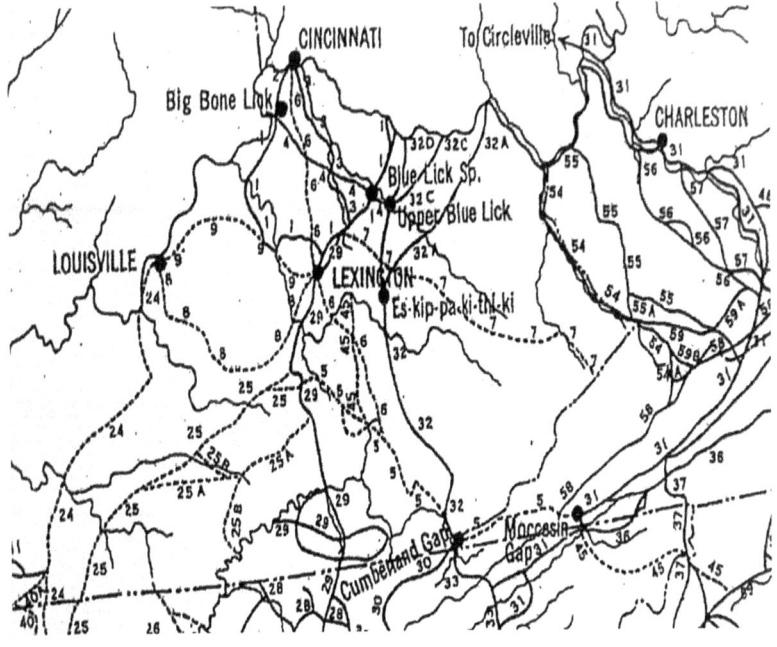

The map above designates the Indian Trails and Buffalo Traces in Kentucky, from the Forty-Second Annual Report of the Bureau of Ethnology to the Smithsonian Institute, 1924-1925. Trail number 32 is the Warrior's Path. At Eskippakithiki the Warrior's Path split into two paths; one designated as path 32A going to the Scioto River in Ohio, and the other going to Upper Blue Lick. The Scioto prong (32A) of the Warrior's Path passed west of Brush Creek in Montgomery County, about 6 miles southeast of Mount Sterling. The Upper Blue Licks prong of the Warrior's Path passed through Mount Sterling, probably at the site of the Little Mountain Indian mound and passed over the Old State Road designated as Path number 7, and likely followed Hinkston Creek for a distance toward Upper Blue Lick. At Upper Blue Lick this prong split again in two; one path being the Salk Lick Creek prong (32C), and the other the Cabin Creek prong (32D). The Cabin Creek prong was selected by the Shawnee Chief Black Fish as the route traveled when the Indians laid siege to Boonesborough in March, 1777.

Indian mound south of Iron Works Road. Adjacent to the left of the mound there was an earthwork ditch for a stockade that was 210 feet in circumference that was supposedly built in 1754. The ditch is still barely discernable in the field. It was also noted that Lucien Beckner dug into this mound in the 1930s, but did not find any burials or artifacts.

View of Pilot's Knob (center of picture) and Goff's Corner (upper left of picture) from the Indian Mound.

View of Howard's Creek looking west from atop of Indian mound.

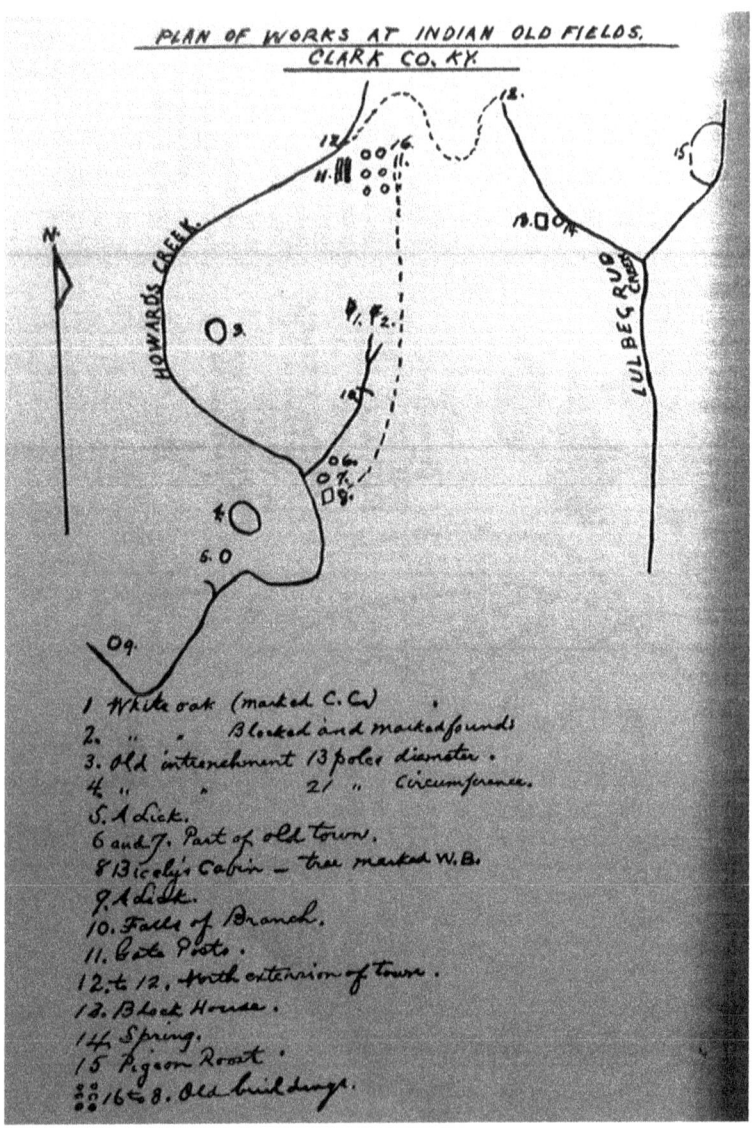

Map of Eskippakithiki from William D. Hixon dated 1886..

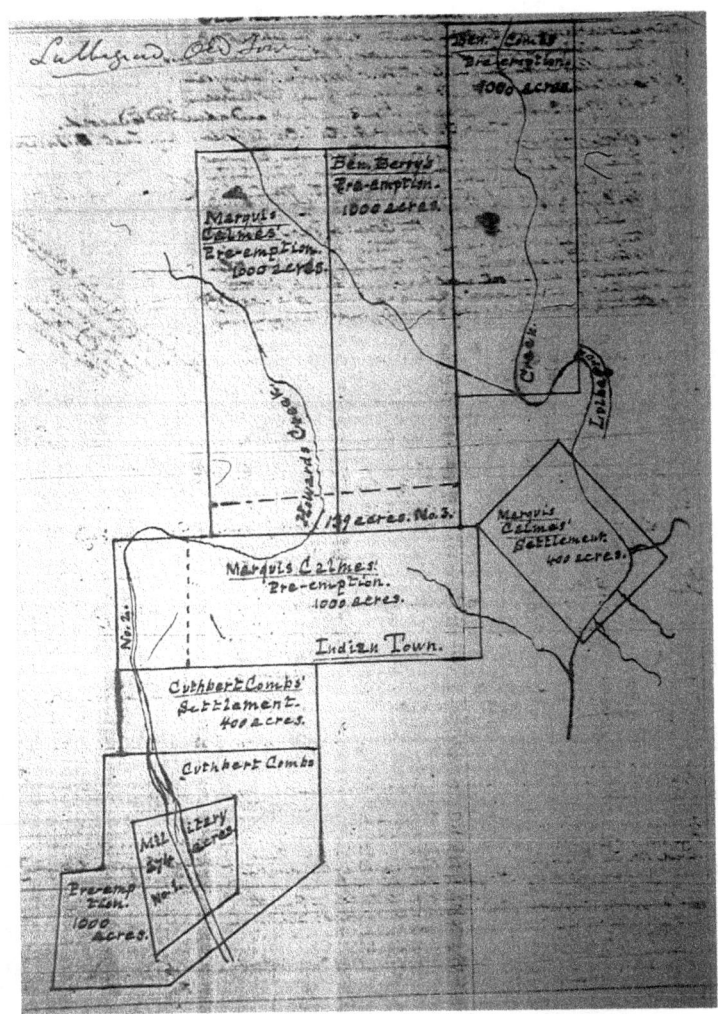

Map from Shane interview with William Risk showing Eskippakithiki land ownership.

View looking west toward site of Indian village and gate posts.

Approximate site of Gate Posts and Indian village on the south side of Mountain Parkway.

Site of a temporary Indian village.

the depth of six inches. There was an old trace that from about Winchester, near by French's – three or four miles to the right of Mt. Sterling, up Slate and out on to the dry ridge." [5]

The Thomas Easton interview by Shane was conducted at Oil Springs in the Indian Old Fields area. "The Indian old fields is a 5000 acre tract, extending from Howard's Upper Creek to Lulbegrud. The gate posts were something near the center. The fields extended over Howard's Creek. The gate posts were on the east side of Howard's Upper Creek, 300 or 400 yards from the bank, in the center of the old fields – a high and very level plain. The posts were in the corner of the orchard, between the old graveyard [Indian Mound?] and the barn. Bluegrass was all over the fields, thickly matted in some places. Many buffaloes. The Indian fortification was near a mile off from where the gate posts were on the other side of the road". [6] Easton also provided an invaluable sketch of his recollections and assumptions on the Indian settlement at the old fields.

Mrs. Thomas Gough lived a short distance from Kiddville on the road to the Red River. She had been in the area for 26 years when Shane interviewed her. "Mr. Gough had seen the gate posts. Only one had an iron band on it. Old Father Gough said when he came here first in 1789 – before Harmer's campaign – the place was covered with the finest buffalo clover; that there was no timber on the place thicker than a man's thigh. Old General Calmes said the cane was so thick you could hardly ride through it. The fort and gate posts were on General Calmes' tract". She then goes on to describe items that were plowed-up, including the bail off a kettle (which they hoped the kettle was loaded with silver, but they never found the kettle) and a stone pipe.[7]

Reverend Shane also interviewed Major Daniels, who lived about six miles from Mt. Sterling at the intersection of the Stone Quarry Road to Kiddville and the Mt. Sterling Road. This would be near the current Clark County / Montgomery County line. He had moved to the area in 1801.

Daniels describes two visits to Indian Old Fields by different Shawnee groups. "Three Indians – one very old, and two younger that were said to be his grandsons – came about here. An old Indian, very gray, tallest Indian I ever saw – no spare flesh about this Indian. They came up through Bourbon, up Grassy Lick and by my place here. Twas said by those who was with them that as soon as they came in view of Pilot Knob, they gave great demonstrations of joy. They were Shawnees. I was there with them some, the night they camped there. I soon found, by his chat, he seemed to be acquainted with the ground he was on. The next day they went on to Red River, about the Pilot Knob." Daniels also describes an Indian visit sometime after the War of 1812. "Some years after the war, the king of the Shawnees and the two boys came about. Their coming this time was procured by Riddle for General David Thompson ... The object of the old man's visit was to keep the place in mind, and he came to show these two Indian boys. They called by here .... I think I got there at breakfast, the king stood and made a speech. Riddle [c] interpreted his speech when he made it. In his speech he told about the country there. Said that they had had a town there till one year before Braddock's war, at the old fields – my understanding is somewhere on Mrs. Gough's farm. That the old man had once lived there. That then some tribe from the south – I think the Catawbas - proving to be too hard for them, they had been obliged to remove way up on Sandy, towards the head of Red River. He also said that a white man, a Frenchman or some European, that was among them had dug that silver mine. That the vein was of the size of a flour barrel and round. [Swift's silver mine]. No such vein was ever found digging. I dug a good deal. The Indians were not at the dig".[8] [Major Daniels is describing the visit of Black Hoof with his two grand-sons at the invitation of Leonard Beall].

    It is evident from these interviews that the initial settlers had seen the remains of an Indian settlement. What the pioneers saw when they first arrived in the Indian Old Fields area may well have been the remains of different and distinct settlements in the same location, and that the location had been occupied for over 2000 years. Not knowing archeology, it would have been easy to assume that all the landmarks were placed there in relatively recent times. But just when was the area inhabited by the Indians? Or was the area inhabited over a long period of time on a temporary basis [d], as a stopping-off point for Indians traveling on the Warrior's Trace? What might have Findley been able to definitively state about Indian Old Fields had any of his writings survived? It is generally accepted by historians that Findley traded with the Indians at Indian Old Fields in about 1767.

What the pioneers were able to identify was:
- That the gate posts were located to the north of Ironworks Road and 200 to 400 yards from Upper Howard's Creek.
- That an Indian village, existing well before the contact period, was located 400 yards to the southwest of the gate posts.
- The earthwork "fort" (possibly a sacred circle) was to the south of Ironworks Road and nearly a mile from the gate posts.
- Adjacent to the earthwork fort is an Indian burial mound.

By triangulating this data on a topographical map, it is possible to ascertain the approximate location of these particular sites noted by the pioneers.

Chisca and the claims of Lucien Beckner
Chisca

In 1955 Lucien Beckner published a manuscript in The Filson Club History Quarterly entitled "The Moundbuilders". In this publication Beckner lays out a case for the Indian village of Chisca actually having been the Indian village of Eskippakithiki. This publication has subsequently been cited in various histories written about Eskippakithiki and Indian Old Fields. Beckner's case is laid out as follows.

In the early 1500s the Spanish had begun explorations of Florida, with Ponce de Leon attempting to colonize Charlotte Harbor in 1521, and Panfilo de Narvaez making a second attempt in 1528. In both cases the Spanish treated the native Indians badly, resulting in a warlike reception to any Europeans. Troubles were later noted in St. Augustine with a hostile group of Indians who were predominately traders, called the Chiscas.

In 1539 Hernando De Soto initiated the conquest and exploration of Florida, taking him from the Carolinas all the way across the Mississippi River. A story is related that in July, 1540, an Indian chief in northern Alabama at a village named Chiaha told De Soto about a land to the north called Chisca, whose people were rich with gold. Beckner stated that De Soto dispatched two soldiers to investigate, and they traveled up the Tennessee River, through the Cumberland Gap, and marched along the Warrior's Path to Chisca, which Beckner claimed is the very site of Eskippakithiki. After 28 days they returned and reported that the country between was so scant of maize and with such high and rough mountains it was impassible for the army, and described Chisca as "a poor, little town where there was nothing of value". [9]

A Portuguese soldier, known as the Gentleman of Elvas, who chronicled De Soto's expedition in the book, Narratives of De Soto in the Conquest of Florida, stated the following: "...that towards the north there was a province called Chisca, and that a forge was there for copper, or other material of that color, though brighter, having a much finer hue, and was to appearances much better, but not so much used, for being softer; which was the statement that had been given in Cutifachiqui, where we had seen some chopping knives that were said to have a mixture of gold. As the country on the way was thinly peopled, and it was said that there were mountains over which the beasts could not go, the Governor [De Soto] would not march directly thither, but judged that keeping in an inhabited territory the men and animals would be in better condition, while he would be more exactly informed of what there was, until he should turn to it through the ridges and a region which he could more easily travel. He sent two Christians to the country of Chisca, with Indians who spoke the language, that they might view it, and were told that he would await their return at Chiaha for what they should have to say". The Gentleman of Elvas further related, "In three days they that went to Chisca got back, and related that they had been taken through a country so scant of maize, and with such high mountains, that it was impossible the army should march in that direction; and finding the distance becoming long, and that they should be back late, upon consultation they agreed to return, coming from a poor little town where there was nothing of value, bringing a cow hide as delicate as a calfskin the people had given them, the hair being the soft wool on the cross of the merino with the common sheep". From a less than certain point of embarkation, the direction traveled by the two soldiers is not clearly stated, and no further details of the travels are stated in the chronicle.

Beckner then turns to the early mapmakers. The Flemish mapmaker Cornelius Wytfliet's map of North America prominently notes Chisca located south of the big northern bend of the Ohio, in what would appear to be the present Kentucky Bluegrass region. Later in 1688, Jean-Baptiste-Louis Franquelin, the official cartographer to the King of France, more exactly located Chisca on his map, apparently in Kentucky between what is today called our Licking River and the Red River. [10]

Records kept by the French Jesuit priests indicate that some of the French were driven out of Illinois by "The Five Nations". The Jesuit Relations of 1670 states that some of the French were driven out of Illinois and fled southeast, taking refuge with the Shawnee Indians at Eskippakithiki. The French-Canadian Census of 1736 stated that the Shawnee village of Eskippakithiki number between 800 – 1000 people.[11]

The Peter Chartier Affair

Lucien Beckner's 1932 article in the Filson Club History Quarterly stated that Eskippakithiki was also the temporary home of Peter Chartier and his band of Shawnee Indians. In the early 1700s the French and the British were actively seeking the support of the many Indian tribes from Canada and New England to the west down the Mississippi valley and in the southern regions to tip the balance of power as these two nations struggled against each other for the control of North America. As the story goes, in 1718 Peter Chartier, the half-Shawnee son of Martin Chartier, was licensed a trader in Conestoga, Pennsylvania and in 1730 married a Shawnee squaw. He instigated secret correspondence with the French against the English, and was accused of the murder of a pro-English Seneca chief. With about 400 Delawares and Shawnees, Chartier drifted down the Ohio River, and Beckner speculated that they took the Warrior's Path south and arrived to Indian Old Fields in May, 1745. Beckner stated that cabins were built in all directions, extending almost a mile northward to Kiddville and a mile eastward to Oil Springs. But the population was impossible to control, eating the stores, driving away the game, and the pro-English Iroquois sought them out and harassed them continually until sometime in 1747 or 1748 they were forced to flee beyond the reach of the Iroquois. [12]

In History of the American Indians, James Adair stated that, "In the year 1747, I headed a company of cheerful, brave Chikkasah [Chickasaw Indians, located in west Tennessee in the Memphis area, who over history were steadfastly loyal to the British], with the eagles tails, to the camp of the Shawano [Shawnee] Indians, to apprehend one Peter Shartee [Chartier], a Frenchman who, by his artful paintings and supine conduct of the Pennsylvanian government, had decoyed a large body of the Shawano from the English, to the French, interest. But fearing the consequences, he went around an hundred miles, toward the Cherokee nation, with his family, and the head warriors, and thereby evaded the danger". As indicated in this passage, by 1747 Chartier's band was well into the Tennessee area and was still being pursued by the British. Even Lyman Draper in his now published manuscript The Life of Daniel Boone relates this story of Chartier and the settlement of Eskippakithiki on Lulbegrud Creek. Yet the evidence is not at all considered conclusive by various historians, despite the enormous respect for the research conducted by Draper.

Current Archeological Surveys and Conclusions
A prehistoric (before the contact period of 1540 – 1795) village site has been identified in an 1986 archeological survey by the University of Kentucky about 400 yards southwest of the gate posts. This village, from the artifacts found, seems to date to around A.D. 1300 to A.D. 1400.

Chisca
In a manuscript submitted to the Kentucky Heritage Council entitled Indian Occupation and Use in Northern and Eastern Kentucky During the Contact Period (1540 – 1795): An Initial Investigation dated March, 1986 by the University of Kentucky Museum of Anthropology, it states that "Lucien Beckner proposed that Indian Old Fields was the site of Chisca, a town visited in 1540 by the Spanish De Soto Expedition. This article has never been seriously considered by professional archaeologists and historians due to the lack of substantive data". Others have argued that the territory of Chisca was on the upper Nolichucky River in Tennessee. Beckner's manuscript lacks conclusive evidence, such as diaries giving first-hand corroborative accounts of the exact location of Chisca, or even detailed geographic data or descriptions of the site. As such, the University of Kentucky manuscript states that Beckner's conclusions have left the association of Chisca with Indian Old Fields in the realm of speculation.

The Peter Chartier Affair
Again the authors of Indian Occupation and Use in Northern and Eastern Kentucky disagree with Beckner and

Draper stating that, "The main reason for placing Chartier in the Indian Old Fields in 1745-46 seems to have been the [scarcity] of data which would suggest that Chartier was anywhere else during that time period". The authors confirm that it is documented that during this time there was a band of Shawnee whose whereabouts were unknown for two years, which historians have used to place Chartier at Indian Old Fields. In addition they note that "15 or 16 [French] Canadians sent in search of Chartier's band by de Longueuil, as requested by the Governor of Canada, found the Shawnees in the lower Scioto River valley where they were clearing fields and setting up residence", and that they were first encountered on June 10, 1745. Based on this, it is certainly questionable that Chartier and his band of Shawnees settled in Eskippakithiki in 1745 as stated by Beckner.

Limited Archeological Surveys

Various professional archeological surveys have been undertaken at the site of the Indian Fort, and the conclusion to date is that there is "no evidence of a major Indian village located at the site, nor has any proof been found to suggest that the area was used by Historic (within the contact period of 1540 – 1795) Indian groups. The most recent survey was conducted by the authors of the "Indian Occupation and Use in Northern and Eastern Kentucky" and this survey identified the earthworks as a sacred circle and earthen mound. These structures are attributed to the Woodland time period, and are believed to display the activities of a cultural group which date between 150 B.C. and A.D. 400. Examination of the artifacts taken from this mound may reveal that the Indians buried in the mound were part of the Adena culture noted prominently in neighboring Montgomery County.

Further, the information from the latest survey would suggest that the site of an Historic Indian Period (1540 – 1795) village lies on the level plain overlooking Upper Howard Creek near where the Mountain Parkway crosses the stream. The evidence suggests that there has been more than one village in the area.

Conclusions

The firm evidence to thoroughly understand Indian Old Fields remains elusive, a victim of budgetary restraints in the archeology departments in Kentucky's various state-funded universities. The elusive nature of firm evidence of the area, while teasing with a few clues from quick surveys and incomplete investigations, leaves enough questions unanswered to allow for authoritative speculation backed with, at best, circumstantial evidence. No exhaustive archeological investigation of the area has been undertaken. And each year the evidence that is sought becomes more difficult to obtain as the rapidly increasing erosion of the original landscape due to the construction of highways, subdivisions and small factories will soon leave little evidence of what was once Indian Old Fields.

Estill's Defeat

In 1831 Chief Justice George Robertson of the Kentucky Court of Appeals said of Estill's Defeat: "It is a memorable incident, and perhaps one of the most remarkable in the interesting history of the settlement of Kentucky. The grief and despondence produced by the catastrophe contributed to give Estill's defeat a most signal notoriety and importance, especially among the early settlers". The impact of this battle has to be understood within the context of the times to be better appreciated today. [a]

Twenty-five year old Captain James Estill was a resident of Boonesborough in 1775, the year of its founding. Captain Estill stood five feet, ten inches with a slender, wiry build. [1] In 1776 Estill took a pre-emption on 1000 acres of land located on the head waters of Muddy Creek and Otter Creek in present Madison County, Kentucky. In 1778 Estill moved his family to Boonesborough. His brother Samuel arrived in 1779, and together in the spring of 1780 they built a cabin on Little Muddy Creek and planted a crop of corn. They then began a stockade or fort on the south bank of the Kentucky River in a heavily wooded area near a clear spring. This site, known as Estill's Station, was located about 15 miles from Boonesborough and about 4 miles east of current Richmond, Kentucky near the Warrior's Trace. The station was always considered to be situated at the most dangerous point in the county.[2]

When the station was ready, about 30 people moved out from Boonesborough to the new settlement. Among those known to be in or near Estill's Station in 1780 – 1781 include James Estill, Samuel Estill, Peter Hackett, Thomas Warren, David Lynch, Nicholas Proctor, Joseph Proctor, John Cattlepool, James Miller, George Robinson, Thomas Miller, Mike Sherley, Green Clay, Adam Caperton, John Colefoot, Captain David Gass, Lt. John Smith, James Berry, William Cradlebaugh, David Cook, and Joseph Rogers. At this time in residence there were about 18 men and 12 women. The first survey of the station was made by Green Clay in May, 1781.

During 1780 and into early 1781 there were continuous incidents with the Indians, with raids and counter-raids launched on large and small scales. Most of the Indian harassment consisted of opportunistic hit-and-run affairs, and were designed at stealing horses from the outlying cabins and stations.

Since the founding of Boonesborough in 1775 the settlers remained mostly "in" their stations, seldom venturing out alone from sight of the station walls. The settlers in nearby cabins would bolt their doors and windows at sunset, and they were not unlocked until well after daybreak. Before venturing out of their cabins, the settlers would first send out the dogs to detect the different scent of any nearby Indians and sound the alarm. Moccasin prints left around the cabins at night became so familiar that the settlers began to recognize the individual Indian by his moccasin print. In future interviews these new migrants consistently used the spatial terms of "settling in" to the confines of the stockades in troublesome times and afterwards "settling out" to nearby farms. [3]

The Muddy Creek area had attracted the settlers from their first arrival at Boonesborough. In the fall of 1775 Daniel Boone had initiated some "improvements" for James Wharton. In the spring of 1776 Joel Walker had constructed a small cabin on Muddy Creek with the help of Richard Epperson. Stephen Hancock, who saw this cabin in 1778, described it as "a small cabin covered with boards, having a mortar in the yard to pound corn, with two acres of ground cleared and planted near the cabin, with a brush fence around it, with a little spring cleaned out near it, with the corn badly worked". [4]

In the spring of 1780, James Estill and John Calloway were undertaking a precautionary reconnoiter in the area of the station looking for signs of Indians, and some 7 or 8 miles from the station they crossed an Indian trail of some 16 Indians heading for the fort. They followed the tracks for several miles and came upon the Indian camp. They carefully studied the encampment while hidden in the tall cane that grew thick throughout the area. Finally, the two men attacked in surprise making as much noise as possible, and the Indians fled their camp in panic, taking only their guns. [5]

    In the spring of 1781 a company of Dutch settlers under Abraham Bantas, who had been encamped at the station for a short time, departed Estill's Station on horseback with their goods traveling on a plain trace toward Mulberry Lick to establish a new fort on Muddy Creek about five miles distant. Escorted by James Estill and his brother Samuel, who in his own right was a noted frontiersman and Indian fighter and was an exceptionally large man, the company had proceeded only about one mile from the station when Samuel discovered a party of Indians concealed. Samuel sounded the alarm, and before James could dismount he was shot in the right arm just above the elbow shattering the bone, and rendering the arm completely useless. Holding his rifle in his left arm, the horse's bridle fell and his horse bolted from the scene. James had extreme difficulty in controlling the horse and remaining mounted, but finally was able to gather the reins with his left hand, and remained disengaged from the encounter.

    Meanwhile, Samuel and the men of the Bantas company returned fire on the Indians, with Samuel shooting two Indians early in the fight. At one point Samuel saw a tall painted savage running toward him with a tomahawk raised in his hand, and Samuel presented himself to the Indian with an ax in his hand, and the Indian upon closer inspection of the size of Samuel Estill, decided against proceeding and fled to the area from which he had started. At this point one of the Dutchmen yelled to Samuel to shoot an Indian rushing at him. Samuel replied, "Shoot him yourself, my gun is empty". The Dutchman shot the Indian at such close range as to leave powder burns on his clothing. Samuel then gathered the company and made an orderly retreat back to the station, and the Indians did not pursue. At the fort it was noted that Samuel's clothing was riddled with bullet holes, yet he did not receive injury. [6]

In October, 1781 British General Cornwallis surrendered his forces to General Washington at Yorktown, Virginia effectively ending the Revolutionary War in the east. But the British continued their efforts against the rebellion, and made every effort to strengthen the northwestern settlements in the Mississippi Valley. In 1782 the British in Detroit incited the various Ohio tribes against Kentucky, with lavish gifts and money to win the good will of the tribes. [7] These Indian tribes included the Shawnees, Miami, Iroquois, Delawares, Wyandotte, Mingoes, and Cherokees.

In 1782 the British conceived a plan with their Indian allies to assemble at the Shawnee's capitol of Chillicothe in August and march in force against the Kentucky stations. The plan included smaller actions by the Indians to keep the settlers "pinned down" south of the Ohio River so that the concentration of forces would not be detected. It was one of these parties that started the bloody warfare of 1782 in Kentucky. In the first days of March a war party made a surprise attack on Strode's Station, killing two men, wounding 16 year-old John Judy (who would later become a founder of Mount Sterling), and killing all the sheep and cattle. The siege lasted a day and a half, and the Indians departed with the horses that they could gather from the settlement. The garrison was too weak to pursue, having just previously sent some men to Boonesborough where an attack was expected. [8]

Early in the day on Saturday, March 19, 1782 an Indian canoe was spotted floating on the Kentucky River past Boonesborough with no one in it. The alarm was raised, and a dispatch sent immediately to Estill's Station and to Colonel Benjamin Logan at his fort, St. Asaph's. From his own station, and from Boonesborough, Miller's Station at Paint Lick, and the surrounding stations Estill raised twenty-five men. Colonel Logan dispatched fifteen men to Estill's Station with orders to search for the Indian party before they could further menace the settlements. With a mounted force totaling 40 men, Estill set out on the evening of the 19th to search for the Indians. They set out eastward toward a point on the Kentucky River near the mouth of the Red River, where Indians were in the habit of crossing with stolen horses. Only Alexander Robertson, who was lying disabled from wounds received from a previous Indian encounter, remained as a defender of the station. Three youths, Peter Hackett, Samuel South and John Gass, completed the number of defenders. That same night the Indian war party arrived to Estill's Station and concealed themselves in the trees and cane within sight of the station. The night was cold, and snow had begun to fall, but the Indians maintained their concealed vigil near the smoldering log piles that were being burned from the trees felled to clear the area around the station. [9] During the course of this same day the Indians had attacked an outlying cabin near the station and killed and scalped a woman and her two daughters. [10]

On Sunday morning, March 20 the station had no indication that they were surrounded, and the routine of the station continued as normal. Monk, the slave of Captain Estill, walked out of the station to the east side and continued his task of hauling cut trees and cane toward the large log piles. Hitching the slide to two horses, he proceeded toward the nearest cut tree. At the same time, another slave, Dick, went from the fort accompanied by Jennie Gass, the 13 year-old daughter of Captain David Gass, toward the sugar camp some 300 to 400 yards on the west side of the station. As Monk approached a brush pile with his first load, the Indians concealed on the other side sprang forth and took him prisoner. The commotion of this incident was noted in the fort, and the cry went out to Dick and Jenny. Both started to run toward the fort, and the Indians rushed forth to intercept them. The surprise of the Indian attack was complete. Seeing this event unfold, cries rang forth from the fort, "Run, Jenny, run"! But the Indians shot Jenny within 60 yards of the fort, and dragging her to a nearby tree within sight of the fort, scalped her. Her little brother, John Gass, who was about a year younger, grabbed a rifle and fired at his sister's murderer. Dick reached the fort safely taking a more circuitous route.[11]

Meanwhile, the Indians who held Monk had decided that he would bring a good bounty from the British and that he would be held a prisoner, and they began to interrogate him about the strength of the station. The loyal slave exaggerated the strength of the station, saying that it was well garrisoned by a strong force, and could easily withstand the attack from the Indians.[12]

As the Indians deliberated the situation, they taunted the defenders in the station with cries of "Run, Jennie, run"! Perhaps discouraged by Monk's report of the strength of the station, the Indians then began to kill all the cattle and, after taking the two horses from the slide, together with Monk the Indians slipped away.

Later in the day when it was thought to be safe to venture out from the stockade, the women sent Peter Hackett and Samuel South on foot to overtake Estill and inform him of the attack. The two boys traveled 18 – 20 miles overnight before finding the party at Estill's Spring near current Irvine, Kentucky the next morning. After giving their excited report, five men who had families at the Station returned to Estill's Station. South and Hackett remained with the scouting party, and the two exhausted boys with the remaining 35 men started immediately down the river to pick up the Indian's trail. The snowfall and wet ground made tracking less difficult, but the Indians made no effort to conceal their direction, leaving as many signs as possible, even pausing their leisurely progress to tap some sugar trees. The party followed the Indians along a buffalo trace all day on Monday, March 21, and camped that night near the Little Mountain Indian mound at current Mount Sterling, Kentucky, not knowing that the Indians had camped less than a mile away.

At daylight the following morning, Tuesday, March 22, Estill assembled the men and addressed them, telling them that they had fighting to do that morning, and requested that every man who did not feel he could fight to remain in the camp. Estill said that he felt more like shooting down a coward who would leave his friends fighting in the battlefield than he did the enemy. [13] Ten men whose horses were too jaded from the rapid marches of the past few days and who therefore could not make good progress were left behind at Little Mountain. Estill then took up the trail with 25 men. [14]

Starting off that dawn in Estill's party were Col. William Irvine, Joseph Proctor and his brother Rueben, James Berry, William Cradlebaugh, David Lynch, Henry Boyer, John Jameson, David Cook, Lt. William Miller [b], Adam Caperton, Jonathan McMillan, Lt. John South Jr., John Colefoot, Michael McNeally, William Crim, Whitson George, Peter Hackett, Beal Kelly, Samuel South, Joseph Rogers, [15] James Anderson, _____ Forbes and _____ Johnson. [16]

Marching rapidly in 4 lines they quickly discovered by the appearance of the Indian track that the Indians were not very distant. Estill and his men were inspired with vengeance at the killing of Jennie Gass, the killing of their cattle and the capture of Monk. Cresting a rise, they found 6 of the Indians at a little distance down the hill, skinning a buffalo on the south side of Hinkston Creek where a buffalo trace crosses the creek. The main body of Indians in the party were already across the creek and advanced a little way north up the next hill. The company was ordered immediately to dismount. Captain Estill fired his rifle "with effect", and the 6 Indians began to move off. David Cook, an impetuous member of the party, who was somewhat advanced, raised his gun and fired at an Indian at the instant that another stepped into range, both being killed by the same shot. [17] This remarkable shot was witnessed by several of Estill's men. This greatly encouraged the pursuers, who then pushed forward descending the slope toward the creek. The Indians, who proved to be Wyandotte's and 25 in total – the same number as Estill's men – were taken by surprise and were disposed to retreat, but their chief

Estill's Defeat

urged them to fight, and they took their stand on the far side of the creek and the engagement began. [18] The ground was highly favorable to the Indian mode of warfare. Thick cane abounded on both sides of the creek, growing more thickly on the hillsides, and the area was heavily wooded.[19]

In the first volley the Indian chief, whose name to this day is unknown, [c] was shot in the creek by a "chance shot",[20] dragged himself behind a bush on the opposite bank and in a loud voice directed the movements of the Indians for the balance of the battle. Two subordinates to the chief in this battle were known to be Split Log, a member of a famous Wyandotte family, and Round Head. Both were actively engaged in the contest. It is presumed that Split Log, only 17 years old at the time, was the warrior with the red leggings who was darting about in support of his comrades and who attracted the attention of Col. William Irvine. [21]

Both parties now took to their trees with only a narrow creek between them, each combatant selecting his adversary. "Each man to his man, and each man to his tree". [22] At the outset three Indians had fallen before returning the first shot. The battle was fought at a bend in the Hinkston Creek that bears northeast, between two small creeks that emptied into the Hinkston Creek from the east. The battlefield reflects the close quarters in which the engagement took place, and only encompassed a couple of hundred square yards with the parties less than fifty yards apart. Jonathan McMillan was killed at the outset of the battle when he started a one-man charge against the enemy, swearing that he would have a shot at an Indian. [23] Estill had taken his position on the south side of the little branch in the center of the battlefield and about 30 yards from Hinkston Creek. John South, John Colefoot, and Michael McNealy were among those closest to Estill. The buffalo trace crossed Hinkston Creek a little south of Estill's position. [24]

Monk had made his escape from the Indians at the first shots, dropping back when the Indians moved off until Estill's force came up to him. He was placed to guard the horses on the left side of the battlefield. Lt. William Miller took up position on the left wing in this area to prevent the Indians from taking the horses.

The battle proceeded in the style of single combat. Each man sought his man, and fired only when he saw his mark. Wounds and death were inflected on each side, but neither side was able to advance or retreat. The firing was deliberate; with caution they looked, but look for the foe they would, although life itself was often the forfeit. And so both sides stood and fell for nearly an hour. Estill was wounded early in the battle, and the loss of blood was beginning to take its toll. [25] Each man had the lingering expectation that death was at hand, and yet they had the courage to fight. [26] After more than an hour of action, with the situation left practically unchanged, and men on both sides being wounded, and powder and bullets running low, neither party could advance or retreat without fatal peril. Estill was well versed with the frontier strategy that, when in a pitched battle with the savages, advantage could be gained by a successful turning of their flank. Estill thus sought an opportunity to make this maneuver. A little valley, flanking and extending to the rear of the Indians' position, suggested the feasibility of such a movement, though only at great hazard, as by weakening the force in front, the enemy might gain the advantage sought by Estill. Finally making the critical decision, Estill directed Lt. William Miller with six men (nearly a third of the able-bodied force) to gain the rear of the savages, while their absence from the line was disguised by an extension of the diminished force which remained. During this time Estill received a second wound.[27]

Miller and his men set out to attempt the flanking maneuver, crossing the creek on the left (south) side of the battlefield, and were fired upon by the Indians who had discovered the movement. Forbes, whose first name is unknown, was killed on the Indians' side of the creek. Some claim that a bullet struck the lock of Lt Miller's gun rendering it inoperable, others say he lost his piece of flint, and still others offer that the thick canebreak prevented him from

Estill's Defeat Road Marker at the corner of Hinkston Pike and Maysville Road.

Estill's battleground is in the wooded area at the bottom of this hill. The spot where Estill fell is under the right hand lane in the picture of I-64 near the green Interstate sign. Picture taken from the Hinkston Pike bridge that crosses I-64 looking west.

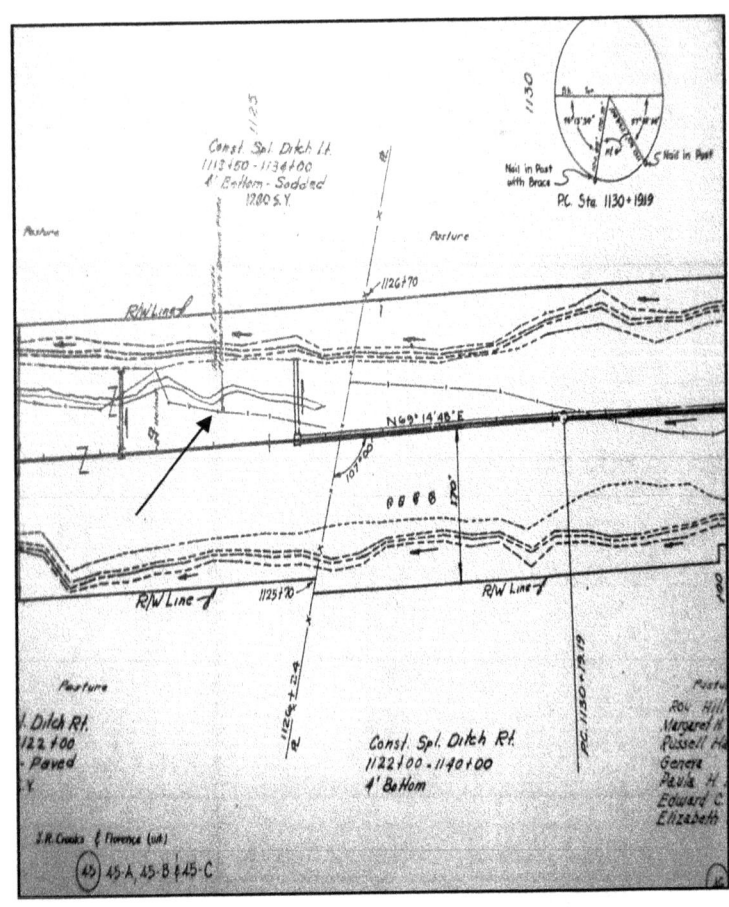

Sheet 53 of 479 from the Kentucky State Highway Department clearly showing where the west bound lane of I-64 covers the spot where Estill fell (see arrow). The small vertical notation says "Rock and Concrete Monument with Brass Plate".

Picture of the battleground of Estill's Defeat taken before the construction of I-64 over this spot. The visible farm road crossing Hinkston Creek is thought to be on the location of the buffalo trace. The fighting would have taken place on the land depicted on the right side of this picture.

Notes to addendum of Survey by Robert Morrow on September 16, 1817 depicting Estill's battleground and noting places where Estill, McNeeley, Smith, Colefoot, and McMillen were killed.

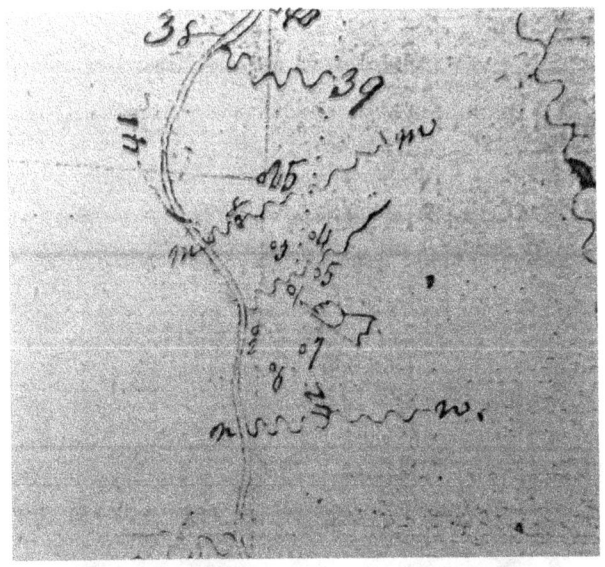

Estill's battlefield from Survey by Robert Morrow on September 17, 1817 showing Hinston Creek and the small branches that fed into the creek where the battle took place. "1" denotes the spot where Estill fell.

Monk, the slave of Captain Estill, became the first slave freed in Kentucky for his valor on the battlefield at Estill's Defeat. Painting by Sallie Chiles Johnston, a descendant of the Estill family. Courtesy of current owner, Katherine V. Dalton.

ABOVE: Monument dedicated November 30, 1932 at site where Estill fell.
BELOW: Brass marker that was attached to the monument.

gaining access to the rear of the Indians. Regardless, he failed to carry out the flanking maneuver and re-crossed the creek when he saw an Indian flanking party approaching and heard firing at his division. Miller ran by Reuben and Joseph Proctor, saying he has lost the flint of his gun, but did not stop when offered another. As he continued his retreat to the south with his four surviving men he also ignored the appeals of Monk, who was with the horses, urging him not to leave the field of battle, as Monk could see the others still fighting. There is no evidence that Miller or any of his men ever fired a shot. Participants in the battle are positive that they did not. [28]

The Indians now saw the advantage gained and the opportunity to launch a counter-attack. With Miller's defection the left wing was unprotected, and an Indian flanking party made an attempt to gain the rear of Estill's forces. Estill ordered Ensign David Cook with three others to occupy the ground that was to have been defended by Miller. One of the three sighted an Indian and shot him, after which they retreated. Cook was in the lead, and after discharging his gun he ran toward a large tree for shelter. Now noting that his three companions were on a small hill, he began to retreat toward them and became entangled in the branches of a fallen tree. With this slight pause he was shot below his shoulder blade and the ball came out at the collar bone.

The main force of the Indians now crossed the creek at the buffalo trace, and Estill continued to fight from his position, now receiving his third wound. In the ensuing fight Michael McNeally, John South and John Colefoot were killed, James Berry was shot through the thigh and _____ Johnson was also wounded. Joseph Proctor called out to Estill that a large number of the men were dead, and he urged Estill to retreat to his position a little further up the hill. Estill agreed to leave the field. His progress towards Proctor's position was slow due to his weakness from the loss of blood. [29]

At this juncture one of Estill's warm personal friends, Adam Caperton, received a ball through the mouth and head, which instead of prostrating him, crazed his brain, and, unconscious of his danger, he began to stagger in the space which still separated the two lines. A powerful Indian, whose gun had just been discharged, sprang forward with his tomahawk to dispatch the unfortunate man. Estill, observing the danger to his friend, and with his gun also being unloaded, rushed forward knife in hand to defend his Adam. Estill and the powerful Indian immediately grappled, and for a time they were evenly matched. [30] Joseph Proctor had been watching the struggle, unable to fire for fear of striking Estill instead of the Indian. His attention became diverted when his brother Reuben yelled for Joseph to kill the Indian pursuing him, which he did with an expert shot. Joseph quickly reloaded and returned his attention to Estill and the Indian. [31] Just then – still wrestling with the Indian, Estill's right arm snapped, having been broken only months earlier from the bullet that passed through his arm just above the elbow at the battle of Muddy Creek, and the savage plunged his knife into Estill's heart. Scarcely had the Indian's yell of triumph told the result of the struggle, when a bullet from Proctor stretched the Indian dead upon Estill's body. [32] Proctor drew the survivors up the hill and regrouped. Colonel William Irvine was shot through the lungs covering this retreat. When the Indians were not able to press the battle any further, they decided to leave the field with their wounded.

    The battlefield now fell silent, and even the voice of the Indian chief, who had animated his followers, was no longer heard. Estill was the last man to fall. [d] Shortly thereafter, the battle stopped by "mutual consent". [33] The length of the engagement has been estimated at an hour and forty-five minutes to 2 hours. [34] Colonel Irvine was mounted on Estill's horse, and James Berry was carried most of the way back to Estill's station on Monk's back. It was a "drawn battle" with both sides inflicting nearly equal losses upon the other. There was a widely circulated tradition that only one of the Wyandottes ever retuned to his village. But the battle is referred to as a "defeat" since the settlers left their dead on the field. [35]

Seven men were left dead on the field of battle: Captain James Estill, Adam Caperton, Jonathan McMillan, Lt. John South, John Colefoot, Michael McNeally and ____ Forbes. It is not known with certainty which of the men "ingloriously" fled the field with Lt. Miller, but these five are certainly among the survivors of the battle. The survivors included: Col. William Irvine, Joseph Proctor, Rueben Proctor, James Berry, William Cradlebaugh, David Lynch, Henry Boyer, John Jameson, David Cook, Lt. William Miller, William Crim, Whitson George, Peter Hackett, Beal Kelly, Samuel South, Joseph Rogers, James Anderson, and ____ Johnson. Of the twelve men who walked off the battlefield at the end, four were wounded (William Irvine, David Cook, James Berry, and ____ Johnson), and Joseph Proctor, Rueben Proctor and six others were able to attend to the wounded with the assistance of Monk. [36 e]

On the third day after the battle a party of 40 to 50 men from Estill's, McGee's, Holder's, and Strode's Stations and from Boonesborough returned to the field to bury the dead. The burial party was surprisingly unprepared, having no axes or tools to dig graves, so they placed the bodies beside fallen trees and covered them with logs and chunks of earth. James Estill and Adam Caperton were buried together, as were Jonathan McMillan and ____ Forbes. The Indians had taken their guns, but there is no evidence that they did other harm. [37]

Estill's Station was for some time afterward the object of Indian vengeance. The Indians made repeated incursions against Estill's Station until as late as 1794. [38]

For over twenty years David Cook watched patiently for William Miller to come to Richmond, swearing he would kill him on sight; but Miller prudently kept away. If he had met the threatened fate, no jury in Madison County would have convicted Cook – so intense was, and to this day is, the admiration for those who fought, and the detestation for those who shamefully retreated from, that most desperate and deadly of all frontier battles. [39]

In August, 1782 the joint Indian and British forces marched into Kentucky and attacked Bryan's Station. The resulting pursuit of the Indians by the settlers to Blue Licks and the terrible ambush and defeat of those Kentucky pioneers marked the last battle against the British in the American Revolution.

Morgan's Station

Ralph Morgan and his father William, accompanied by a party of gentry from Berkley County, Virginia (now Jefferson County, West Virginia) including the Swearingen brothers – Thomas and Benoni – and Ralph's uncles Michael Bedinger and John Strode, reached Boonesborough in April, 1779. Ralph's grandfather was an early settler to West Virginia, and at the time of their migration to Kentucky the Morgan's were a wealthy, well-respected family. Despite the drama of the American Revolution, they were drawn to the western lands and the adventure of the frontier.[1]

Daniel Boone was not present when the Morgan party arrived to Boonesborough, having returned to North Carolina to bring his family to the fort. What the Morgans found upon their arrival at Boonesborough was a fort greatly weakened by the 12-day siege the previous September by the Shawnee Chief Black Fish and 440 Indians. After the siege several families returned to their homes in the east, and the fort was under the command of Captain John Holder and about fifteen men. The Morgan party remained at Boonesborough throughout the summer and significantly strengthened its numbers of defenders. They found the fort operating under a communal system where meat and food was openly shared with all the inhabitants, and they spoke freely of their concerns for their safety and their plans for the future.

Jacob Myers was of Dutch descent and worked with survey crews involved in claiming lands in Kentucky. He had money and by 1779 was starting to acquire what land he could. His timing could not have been better, because the following year would bring a flood of immigrants to the Kentucky region. Early on by dubious means Myers successfully claimed a large tract of land along the Ohio River, and continued gathering land claims until at one point he had claimed over 185,000 acres – a tract slightly larger than current Fayette County, Kentucky. Among his land holdings were some 40,000 acres along the Slate Creek in Bath and Montgomery Counties. On these lands along Slate Creek were discovered ore deposits, and promptly the first ironworks furnace west of the Allegheny Mountains was built.[2]

Ralph Morgan participated in Bowman's retaliatory raid on the Shawnee villages along the Little Miami River in the summer of 1779. The raid had little effect on the Shawnees, who put up a stiff defense of their villages. The Bowman party withdrew from the attack in a disorderly fashion, crossing the Ohio River and returning to their settlements.

That winter John Strode made plans to settle on his 1,000-acre claim along Strode's Creek. He promised land to anyone who would help him build the station. By April of 1780, with the help of Ralph Morgan and others, he founded the well-stockaded fort known as Strode's Station in current Clark County, Kentucky and in 1780 there were some thirty families at the station.

In 1785 Ralph married Mary Douglas, described by one who attended the wedding as "a pretty young Irish widow", the widow of John Douglas who was killed at the battle of Blue Licks in 1782. Mary's maiden name was Bryan, and she was related to Daniel Boone's wife, Rebecca Bryan.

In 1786 Ralph obtained a 5,000-acre tract of land along Slate Creek from Jacob Myers. This land had originally been granted to Myers under treasury warrant No. 742 signed by Governor Patrick Henry of Virginia on December 2, 1785. It is thought that Ralph traded some land he had claimed in Bath County along the Slate Creek (which likely helped consolidate Myers' land holdings around his ironworks) for a more favorable settlement site along Slate Creek in Montgomery County. The ironworks was seven miles further into the frontier from Morgan's new land at the edge of Montgomery County. It would appear that Myers and Morgan jointly planned their ventures under the assumption that two settlements in the area would be safer than one.[3]

Morgan's Station

In February, 1789 Ralph Morgan accompanied the first settlers to the site of the proposed new station, although Ralph had no intention of settling there at this time. The party of men, remarkably well selected for establishing a settlement, included Tom Montgomery, a Revolutionary War veteran, Josiah (Si) Hart, one of the first trustees of Winchester, George Naylor, Robert Dougherty, one of the first justices of Montgomery County, Peter Hanks, who served in the militia on the Pennsylvania frontier during the Revolutionary War, William Hanks, son of Peter Hanks, and James Douglas, a member of the first Kentucky surveying party that was led by Thomas Bullitt in 1773. They selected a sight on a high bluff on the southern perimeter of Harper's Ridge, about fifty yards northwest of a natural spring (near where the old stone house now stands). The spring still flows today. It was a natural defensive position protected on three sides by the steep slope of the bluff, overlooking Slate Creek. Harper's Creek flowed parallel to the ridge to the west, and Slate Creek loops around to the south and east sides. The men staked their claims, and began clearing the land of the overgrowth of cane, Kentucky's native bamboo (*arundinaria gigantean*), which is an evergreen that grows to sixteen feet tall and several inches in diameter. They then planted nearly forty acres of Indian corn, and constructed three cabins in the form of an unfinished rectangle. With their labors completed, the men agreed to return in June to tend to the corn. [4] Yet with the heavy woods the station was nearly concealed from view along the road.

#

James Wade was born in 1770 in Greenbriar County, Virginia (now West Virginia) on the western slopes of the Allegheny Mountains. Because there was no militia in the area, the Indians were attacking the outlying cabins without fear of retribution, and so the Wades retired from their mountain home to the other side of the mountains. In 1784 the Wade family passed into Kentucky through the

Cumberland Gap in a party of some three hundred people, and arrived unmolested by the Indians to McGee's Station in Clark County, Kentucky, which is less than three miles from Boonesborough and on the main trail to Strode's Station. It was there that James would have met William Sudduth and Ralph Morgan, with whom he would have a life-long association.

John Wade, James' older brother, was already working with William Sudduth by 1786. William Sudduth was making surveys in the area of what is now Mount Sterling, and the following is related from Lucian Beckner's "Sketch of Early Adventures of William Sudduth in Kentucky" published by the Filson Club. Sudduth says, "On the second of September (1786) I started out to make a number of Surveys. On the third I made a Survey near where Mount Sterling now stands. It began to rain in the afternoon. Some hunters the winter before had built a half faced camp on the branch that passes through Mount Sterling and about where there was afterwards a tanyard. A plain hunting trace led up the hollow passing by the Little Mountain. Just before we came to the Little Mountain we discovered a fresh trail in the weeds. The men went on to the half-faced camp to stay all night. I seated myself on the Small Mountain to watch the back track. John Wade returned to me and assured me it was Indians, that they had been chewing the green cornstalks which had come up volunteer and that he set his foot in the mud where they crossed the branch and that their tracks looked as fresh as his did. He remained with me until dark. We then went to the camp and I proposed that if we stayed there we should keep guard. The weeds and cane were very high and thick. The trace crossed the branch about ten steps from the Camp. As soon as it was dark I placed a sentinel at the point where the trace crossed the branch and let him remain about two hours. I then directed John Wade to go and relieve him, to go out openly in an opposite direction until he got out of the light of the fire and then take a circuit to where the sentinel was placed, relieve him and direct him to return to camp in the same manner, so

Morgan's Station

that if the Indians were in view that they might supposed it to be the same man. When the sentinel first placed out came in he said he believed there was a raccoon or something else in the branch, that he had heard it sneeze several times. Wade had not set half an hour before he called out "here they are!" and ran into the camp. We snatched up what we could and ran about thirty yards, got out of the light of the fire and stopped. We then went a small distance into the cane and weeds and stayed all night."

On June 2, 1789 eighteen year-old James Wade set out from Strode's station, hired by Morgan as an Indian "spy", as scouts were called in those days, and a hunter in the company of the party of men returning to Morgan's Station. Peter Hanks decided against returning to the settlement, and James Douglas had died. The others did return, and when they reached the station they found that a flock of turkeys had eaten nearly all of the corn. They then sent back to Strode's Station for some seed corn, and William Hanks replanted it. Unfortunately, an early frost destroyed the crop before it could ripen.[5]

Plans to return that fall with their families quickly evaporated as the lack of food for the settlers and their animals would require postponing the inhabitation of the settlement for another year. Since no one would be moving out in the fall, Ralph Morgan turned the place over to James Wade and his brother, John. Their only neighbors were Peter and John Harper, who had arrived to Boonesborough in 1779 and accompanied Enoch Smith to survey land that same year in the area of Montgomery County where they claimed 400 acres. But due to the remoteness of the site, the Harper brothers had not settled their claim until 1789 when Morgan began his station. It was in the spring of 1789 when the Harper's built their cabin four miles to the west of Morgan's Station along the creek that now bears their name. And they remained in their cabin when the party of men left Morgan's Station in the early winter of 1789.

Soon thereafter in the fall the Indian presence was felt again. As James Wade tells the story, "My brother had gone out to hunt a good place to dig ginseng. It was a good time to dig with frost on the ground. He said the first thing he knew, he came on a party of Indians so near that, as he glanced his eyes, he saw their cooking spits sticking all around the fire. The Indians jumped to their guns. He said they were firing on him all the way. He had seven bullets in his hunting shirt without touching his skin, one in the pommel of his saddle, one in the butt of his gun just below the box, and one in the sheath of his hunting knife, cutting off the point of the knife. Thus, he received the plain traces of ten balls. Two Indians followed for a quarter of a mile. He gained none on them that he could see. But at length, despairing of overtaking him, both the Indians fired." [6] John made his escape back to the unmanned station.

The year 1790 began with more cabins being raised in Montgomery County. Enoch Smith, a land surveyor who reputedly knew more about the area than anyone else, and on whose land Mount Sterling would be built, established his station a few hundred feet east of current Maysville Road on Hinkston Road. John Baker built his station further west where US 60 crosses the Clark County / Montgomery County line. On June 29 four Indians attacked several hunters returning at night from Grassy Lick, killing one and wounding another before they could enter the station. These same Indians then proceeded along toward Morgan's Station, where the next morning James Wade discovered their fresh tracks in Harper's Creek. John Wade and Harry Martin were at this time serving as scouts for the ironworks, and they picked up fresh tracks of ten to twelve Indians. They left with a party of ten men to warn James at Morgan's Station, but James had just left to pick up a fresh horse for plowing at his brother-in-law's in Clark County. The Indians ambushed the company near the station, shooting John Wade through the hip.

Ralph Morgan tried to enlist more settlers for his station, and in the spring of 1790 four men – John Handley, Enoch Knox, John Hasty and William Warren – came out but did not stay long enough to even plant corn. They judged the risk of Indian attack to be too great. Lack of stockading may have been a factor. In three or four days they had sold their provisions and returned.

By the fall of 1790 the Wade brothers, John now mobile from his wound to the hip, and James fresh from additional adventures with the Indians, returned to Morgan's Station to harvest the corn crop. They found that a portion of the unattended corn had been trampled by the buffalo and eaten by the bears, yet yielded a good return. Setting aside what would be needed for the settlers expected in the spring, and sharing what they could with the men at the ironworks, the Wades completed their farming tasks for the winter and proceeded to trap beaver along the Red River. [7]

The Northwest Ordinance, passed by the Congress in 1787 after first providing for the survey of the land west of the Appalachian Mountains, established a Governor of the Northwest Territory (then considered to include Ohio, Indiana and Illinois). The Governor had many powers, including the discretion "to lay out the part of the district in which the Indian titles shall have been extinguished, into counties and townships, subject however to such alternations as may thereafter be made by the legislature". As implemented, this gave the Federal Government the ability to secure Indian lands northwest of the Ohio River by force. The result, along with a flood of new immigrants to the Indian territories, was a general renewal of Indian war in the early 1790s. By 1791 the tide of immigrants had reach Montgomery County. As James Wade noted, "The country all around began to be pretty thickly settled".

Several new stations were founded in the neighborhood of Morgan's Station. Nicholas Anderson established Anderson's Station on the dividing range between Lulbegrud Creek and Hinkston Creek (between current Kiddville Road and Tonkin Road near the Levee Road). Thomas Montgomery established Montgomery's Station at the head of Stepstone Creek near the junction of Stepstone Road and Howard's Creek Road. (Thomas later married Martha Crockett, a first cousin of Davy Crockett). Peter Fort built

Fort's Station about two miles east of Morgan's Station. And John Troutman established Troutman's station near the mouth of Peeled Oak on Slate Creek. John immediately sold the station and land to his brother Peter. [8]

Ralph Morgan finally had some luck in 1791 in bringing families out to settle at Morgan's Station. The first to arrive were John Pleake's and Abraham Becraft's families in February. Pleake would stay a year and then go on to establish his own settlement. In March Jacob Allington's family and Peter Curtright's families followed. James Wade was there, and noted that these "were the first families ever there". Other families followed, including those of William Arthur, Daniel Deron, Harry Martin, and Robert Craig. Additional settlers included Rueben Cofer, John Irvine, Andrew Duncan, Solomon Skaggs, and James and John Wade. In all there were about 30 people at Morgan's Station during the year. [9]

Several weeks after Pleake and Becraft brought their families out to Morgan's Station, James Wade said, "the Indians came and found us," and on March 2nd "my brother was killed a short distance this side of the beaver pond that was about a mile below now Iles Mill on Licking". The Indians ambushed John Wade as he rode from the station to the beaver pond to set out his traps. He apparently escaped the site of the initial contact and had gotten about a hundred yards down the trail, when they shot his mare and she fell. He then tried to run but had not gotten far "when a ball struck him in the back of the head".

The Indians backtracked on the trail John Wade had taken, which brought them to Morgan's Station. James Wade said, "From this on they dogged us for two weeks". There were only five men at the station – Rueben Cofer, Andrew Duncan, John Pleake, Abraham Becraft and James Wade. They immediately started to work turning the strongest of the three cabins into a blockhouse. They removed the roof and put on another story. Wade recalled, "Never men worked harder than we did that day, expecting an attack …. Finished that evening chinking and daubing, and all the families came into it. Next day we went to work on another cabin to make another blockhouse". These blockhouses were at the northeast and southwest corners. As soon as they were finished, the men began picketing, or stockading, the station. [10]

Four days later in the late afternoon, a man named Reynolds was shot by an Indian about a quarter of a mile from the station. Wade heard the shot from the station. "On hearing the gun, I ran out from the cabin where I was, and my dog ran towards the fire. When he seemed to have gotten out there, he raised a most powerful bark. We knew it was Indians". Later the men discovered that the Indian had stripped Reynolds of his buckskin pants and one boot. The Indian evidently had been spooked when the dog ran out barking. It was determined that the Indian who shot Reynolds had used John Wade's gun. [11]

Indian troubles continued into the spring of 1792. As William Sudduth stated, "The Indians did mischief within seven miles of me (he built a cabin within two miles east of Hood's Station) that spring and were very troublesome about the Ironworks (on Slate Creek in Bath County) and on the frontier generally".

On June 1, 1792 Kentucky was admitted as the 15th state of the Union. The population had grown sufficiently over the past couple of years to allow the people of the area to petition the government to form a new state. President Washington accepted the petition for the separation of Kentucky from Virginia. During this period of time the efforts of Enoch Smith and Hugh Forbes, whose property lines were marked by the Little Mountain Indian mound, began to bear fruit as more people were willing to settle in the area. Hugh Forbes laid out small lots along Hinkston Creek on what is now Locust Street and began to sell the lots. John Judy purchased 100 acres from Enoch Smith, and this land adjoined the land held by Hugh Forbes, which is to say it was located in the center of the current town. John Judy immediately set out lots and began to sell them. Enoch Knox and Robert Moore built on Smith's land. Robert Walker,

Arthur Connelly and Joe Simpson built the next earliest houses at Mount Sterling. Enoch Smith's and Hugh Forbes' land joined at the mound. [12] [a] On December 6, 1792 the Kentucky Legislature approved, at their second meeting, the creation of Clark County from Fayette County. On December 17th the legislature established Mount Sterling as the first town in Clark County. The settlers near Strode's Station wanted their Station to be the county seat of the new county, and looked unfavorably on the formation of Mount Sterling.

Regarding how the new town received its name, John Crawford states that, "I was present when they had the naming of the town. Enoch Smith proposed that it should be Little Mountain Town (in honor of the historic Indian mound at the site). But Forbes said no, it should be Mount Stirling. He had come from a town in Scotland named Stirling. Forbes ruled, as it was he that began the town". The spelling of the name was almost immediately corrupted by the State Legislature, and the mis-spelling of "Mount Sterling" has remained.

#

The news that Kentucky had been admitted as "one of the fires of the Union" reached the Shawnee villages in northern Ohio. White Wolf knew that this meant the end of their traditional hunting grounds, and any hopes of reclaiming it were gone. Yet, a certain nostalgia tugged at him, and he wanted to have a last look at the abundant hunting grounds.

White Wolf was 52 years old, and had earned the respect of the Shawnee as a warrior. He had been engaged in raids in the New River Valley in 1758, Pontiac's War at Detroit in 1763, the battle of Bushy Run 25 miles east of Fort Pitt in 1763, the battle of Greenbriar Valley in 1763, and numerous raids in the Ohio Valley. He had a fine wife by the name of Shawnee Woman, and three children – now all adults – John Jr., Sutawnee, and Joseph. [13]

White Wolf had been born in about 1741 as John Ward, and at the age of 3 was captured and adopted by the Shawnee. He remembered very little of his white heritage, and now that memory was all but gone. At the large battle of Point Pleasant, White Wolf had unknowingly fought against his father, Captain James Ward of the Army of Virginia, who died in that battle (in The Frontiersmen, Allen Eckert claims that White Wolf actually shot and killed Captain Ward), as well as his brother William.

For many years now it had been too dangerous to take women across the Ohio River into Kentucky. But White Wolf's daughter, Sutawnee, who was the wife of Stand-In-Water, had not seen the Kentucky hunting grounds for about twenty years, and she too wanted a last look. She was now 32 years old, and she felt that this would be her last chance. As plans began to develop for a hunting trip into Kentucky, Sutawnee persisted with her father until he relented and allowed her to accompany the warriors. Eventually the hunting party would consist of about thirty-six Indians from various tribes that were in the area. In early March, 1793 they set out for a final look at the Kentucky hunting grounds.

After crossing the Ohio River and carefully avoiding detection, the band of Indians, with White Wolf, Sutawnee, Stand-In-Water, and others hunted for a couple of weeks, and began working their way north to return to their village as they reached Slate Creek. But everything had changed. They had not yet seen one buffalo or elk. They saw two very skittish deer, and only one black bear. No panthers or wolves were seen at all. And the landscape had all been changed. The unbroken forests and canelands were now plowed fields and cabins and towns. The warriors felt a frustration and anger over what had been done to the land, and the lack of game for the hunt. It was with this anger and hatred for what the white man had done to their land that the warriors came across Morgan's Station. [14]

#

With the Indians being pushed further north in the Northwest Territory, settlers continued to pour out of the stockaded forts and into the unsettled areas of current Clark County, Montgomery County and Bath County. With Mount Sterling established and Morgan's Station continuing to grow in population, people were even moving out from these settlements to claim their own lands. John Pleake moved into his own place on Harper's Creek, a mile and a half west of Morgan's Station. Dawson Wade, James Wade's father, settled near Pleake, less than a mile from the Station. Thomas Hansford established a station on Slate Creek called Peeled Oak. Those moving out of Morgan's Station to take up their own claims included Jacob Allington and Peter Curtright, leaving behind "old Mrs. Allington" who was Jacob's mother and Peter's mother-in-law. David and Jonathan Allington were living on Harper's Creek within a mile of Morgan's Station. Abraham Becraft with his wife and seven children moved out of the station, but only about four hundred yards northeast, to a cabin at the end of the corn field. Andrew Duncan moved in with Becraft. James Wade moved out of the Station to his parent's cabin nearby. The remaining residents of Morgan's Station included Mrs. Allington and four families – those of Robert Craig, Harry Martin, Alexander Baker and Joseph Young.[15]

With so many people in the area, and with no major Indian troubles in the past six months, the residents of Morgan's Station came to believe that they would no longer have worries about Indians. This feeling caused them to become very careless. During the late winter of 1792 / 1793 they had taken down the stockading and the gates and used the defenses for firewood. The men no longer carried guns with them when they moved outside of the Station to tend to the abundant corn fields, wheat fields, cattle and horses. The horses were raised for personal use and farming as well as for sale and trade. The horses were also highly desired by the Indians who would steal them from outside the stations and cabins. One pioneer said that the Shawnee stole so many horses that it seemed that the whites were raising them for the Indians. Men were no longer actively engaged as scouts looking for Indian signs. Life, it seemed, was becoming more "settled". [16]

On Easter Sunday, March 31, 1793 there were nearly one hundred people assembled at Morgan's Station to hear Reverend Hansford preach, the first preaching ever done within 25 miles of Morgan's Station. James Wade again is nearly the only eye-witness to the following events that has been recorded. He said that on that Sunday there were no more than four or five guns at Morgan's Station. Daniel Deron, who lived at Grassy Lick, spent Saturday night at the Station. Sunday morning he and Andrew Duncan were out looking for some lost horses and came across fresh Indian tracks at the narrows of Slate Creek. Deron immediately headed for home, stopping along the way to warn Pleake that there were Indians in the area. The presence of Indians was apparently not considered a threat at Morgan's Station, since no one took any precautions. By this time White Wolf and his band had camped about five miles away at the head of Little Slate Creek (two miles south of Hope on Ky 713). They probably spent the day scouting the station and devising a plan of attack. [17]

As James Wade tells the story, on the following morning, Monday, April 1st, "Reverend Hansford had been to my father's when I was not at home, and told my mother he wanted some corn (for his new station), and me to come up immediately, as soon as I got home. And not knowing when I would be in – they didn't wait for me. The crib of corn was up at the station, and I had a little stable just fixed up at the end of Morgan's Station. As soon as I came in, my mother told me, and I rode right on up to the station. Before this, they had gone on, gotten their corn, shelled and measured it, and had started home with it. I turned my horse into the little stable, took out the bit, gave him a few ears of corn, and went into Harry Martin's house where I was well acquainted. I was just about to set down, and Mrs. Martin handed me a chair, saying 'I've got some money for you' [for the corn] when the alarm was raised, and we both ran out.

Martin delayed to jerk down his gun and I got out first. The Becrafts and Andy Duncan had been out at work in the corn fields, and were flying before the Indians – all except Abraham Becraft, the father, who being pretty close to the woods, jumped over the fence and made his escape. The moment we went out we saw the Indians, but Martin thinking there were but two or three ran with all his might in that direction with his gun in hand to relieve the pursued. I called for them to all get into the block houses, sought about for a gun, not knowing, or having had time to know, the actual condition of the station. There were two blockhouses that I had expected them to go in to – but all the women and Joe Young following. There was but one gun, and that Joe Young had. All the others the men having taken with them (who were gone away) into the fields".

"I now looked out through a port hole and saw an Indian in advance carrying a beautifully finished rifle in one hand, the polished brass on the butt glittering as it caught the rays of the sun, and in the other a shining tomahawk brandished over his head. Suddenly, he fell on one knee and aimed a fire at Martin, [who was] running straight ahead within fair reach of him. I wouldn't have wished a prettier shot than a man so running [but the Indian apparently missed]. Some 10 or 15 steps behind followed thirty or forty Indians, all spread out in a line and making towards the station. Martin, startled at seeing how many there were, had turned back and was running with the Becrafts and Duncan before them".

A fire, [just] as ineffectual, from the whole line followed that of the chief. They then raised the yell. As soon as Young heard the firing and the yells, he jerked open the door and ran out. His wife caught him and clung to him, but he loosed her hold and broke away from her grasp. I saw Young pitch up on all fours. I thought he was wounded or shot, but he had only stumbled. [He had] knocked his hat off, but he picked it up again and continued straight on. He and Andy Duncan, who, when he got in [the station] had kept on running through [the other side], got together and made their escape to Anderson's Station up above Mount Sterling. They there had represented that there were 150 to 200 Indians ... and the frightful account of the number of Indians prevented speedy relief, and they would have been afraid to come". Young had left the blockhouse with the only gun.

Now panic had set in, and the remaining women and children began to flee. The Indians were waiting for them. Almost all were captured.

Harry Martin's family were the only ones to escape intact. As Wade relates, "Martin came along, in the juncture of general flight, took out his butcher knife and cut loose his wife's petticoat. He picked up the elder child and, pointing to the younger, told his wife to take it up and follow him. Wheeling a little to the left as they went out on the lower side (south side of the station), they soon got under the hill and were out of sight over Slate. He crossed over Slate at the mouth of Little Slate and said he stayed the night at Peeled Oak. If he had been pursued they would have gotten his wife and children with him. When he got to Montgomery's next morning, he had to leave his wife out some distance till he should go in and get clothes for her". Wade continues, "Old Mrs. Allington, mother of Clarinda Allington, who was then living at the station, went along with Martin as far as she could go, and when overcome with fatigue, laid down till night overtook her and then made her way to Pleak's". The story is told that Mrs. Allington got into a hollow poplar tree and hid until the Indians passed her by, and then made her way during the night to Pleak's by the light of the burning station.

Robert Craig ran from the fort with two Indians chasing him. They outran Craig, but just before they caught up with him, he came to a steep bank on Slate Creek. Without pausing to think, he jumped off the bank, landing on a rock in the creekbed about twelve feet down. His startled pursuers gave up the chase and Craig escaped. Craig left behind his wife and two children. [18]

James Wade now found himself alone and unarmed in the blockhouse, and the Indians starting to set fire to the cabins. "I would have stayed in the blockhouse with just one gun. The burning of the station, I think, would not have set this [blockhouse] on fire unless the wind happened to be unfavorable. They were some feet off. Finding the blockhouse deserted, I ran to the stable to catch my horse. The stable made part of the fort wall. I had my hands twice on his mane, but he was so frightened. I thought if I remain there much longer to catch him the Indians would certainly have me. When I got home, he was there before me. I ran right across the fort to the lower side, with Baker but a step or two before me. I am confident that I was the last person that ran out". He goes on to say, "My escape and freedom from injury was remarkable".

Wade describes his escape, "The Indians, whom I had thought had all gone on one side, seemed to have divided their forces at the north side about equally and came round so as nearly to meet us as we ran out. Indeed I wondered at the Indians, that they had not killed some of themselves in pouring their volley upon us, they seemed to fire so carelessly. Some were in about ten steps of me, and the women and children were flying in every direction. Baker was a big fat Dutchman. It was impossible that he should have escaped. I thought if I could get before him, it might possibly save me some. Just then he came tumbling down with a very heavy fall, right before me. Not ten steps beyond him the firing seemed sharper than ever. I afterwards counted nine bullets that had been shot into a while oak stump which I was just then desiring to throw between them and me".

The Indians killed Baker as soon as he went down. "Two Indians pursued about a quarter of a mile to the creek, but finding that they were distanced, returned to the spoil" [at the station]. James Wade had run through a gauntlet of bullets completely untouched.

"When I ran, crossed Slate Creek below the mouth of Spencer and then Little Slate [and continued] through now

Jefferson Botts's place. Kept too far out to strike Peter Fort's. I took round and went down to Troutman's Station to give them the word, lest the Indians come upon them unawares .... From there I wheeled upon Stepstone Creek and gave the first information at Montgomery's Station, where I knew were some good soldiers. Then came around to my brother-in-law Pleak's on my way to my father's. When I got to Pleak's I found the whole country round about there had gone to Mount Sterling. I heard that they had [been] to my father's and didn't go there. Didn't get my gun till the next morning. My mother had taken my rifle and was on her way with it to Mount Sterling and, understanding that I had been killed, would let no one have it. Two or three men told me that they had met her and asked for it. She said I was killed and what was the use of taking the gun [to me]. Abraham Becraft [had gone] to my father's and told them that he had seen me jump into his wheat field and that, as I jumped, the Indians fired a volley upon me and shot me and that two Indians had jumped over upon me. This he said he saw".

    White Wolf and the warriors pursued and gathered up all the women, children and men left behind. They then proceeded to gather up all the trophies that they could find. Horses, clothing, blankets and bedding, furniture, and tools – anything that was easily moved was taken. They then took their vengeance on the animals that they could not take with them, shooting with arrows the geese, cows, calves and dogs that could be found in the area. They did not necessarily try to kill them, but inflicted pain by wounding many of the larger animals and leaving them to die a slow death. And when all that they could take was gathered, they set fire to all the cabins and blockhouses. White Wolf knew that they could expect to be pursued as soon as a force could be gathered in the area, and that they had to cross the Ohio River as quickly as possible before the famous Indian fighter Simon Kenton (whose real name was Simon Butler) – known as Bahl-der to the Shawnee – could be alerted and put on their trail. Simon Kenton lived near Limestone (current Maysville, Kentucky) and was commonly known on site by the Shawnee. The Indians would make every effort to avoid Kenton as they crossed the Ohio River in that area. This meant they had to travel quickly, and the captives who were too slow or too loud would be killed on the trail.

Later in the day, on Monday, April 1st, men began to gather at Pleak's cabin, which was about 2 miles from Morgan's Station. When they had a sufficient number, they set out to reconnoiter the area. James Wade was among them. They arrived to Morgan's Station after dark. "We went very carefully and didn't at all go up to the fires.... The women had their calves in a little pen, one end of which was made up by my crib. Handy for the cows. These calves were all riled up, not [from] the guns, but [from] the arrows that were left sticking in them. Every goose in the place was shot in the same way. The station was burnt, and my crib was left unharmed. Was build then three years. Was dry and full of dry corn. Everything else was burned. They carried off all the moveable plunder, such as clothing, bedsticks, etc., and gotten every creature (horse) in the place except mine".

The news of the attack spread quickly to the other settlements, and soon a militia was being formed to pursue the Indians. As James Wade relates, "The next morning (2nd of April) by 8 or 9 o'clock they were assembled, some from as far away as Bourbon, to the number of at least one hundred fifty, and pursued under Enoch Smith (then a militia Captain)". There were nearly as many dogs present. The Indians had almost a day's head start, and they were moving quickly. It was easy to pick up the track of such a large group, and Smith's men began the pursuit, knowing the risk to the captives of causing the Indians to move too quickly. Indians were known to kill any captives that slowed their retreat or could not keep up. Still, the raid could not go unanswered.

The savagery of the Indians soon became shockingly apparent to Smith's militia. "When we had gotten about five miles (just above the head of Little Slate)", James Wade continues, "we found Mrs. Becraft and her suckling child (6

ABOVE: *Looking north at stone house at Morgan's Station site built by Andrew Swearinigin in about 1796.*

BELOW: *Beyond this tree looking south from the stone house would be the location of Abraham Becraft's cabin. The field was planted in corn. The Indians approached from the ravine to the right.*

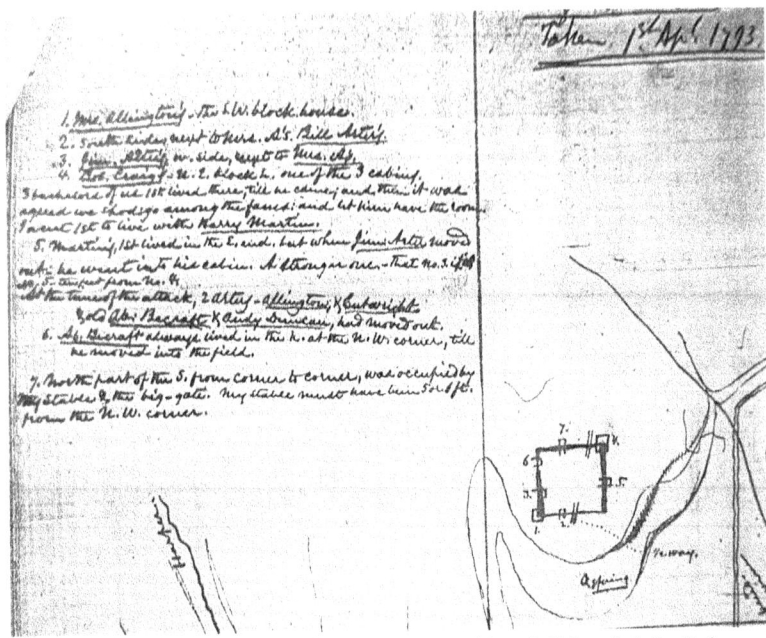

ABOVE: Notes from Shane's interview with James Wade showing Morgan's Station prior to the attack.
BELOW: Morgan's Station and Becraft's cabin. The Indians approached from the ravine at Slate Creek near Becraft's cabin.

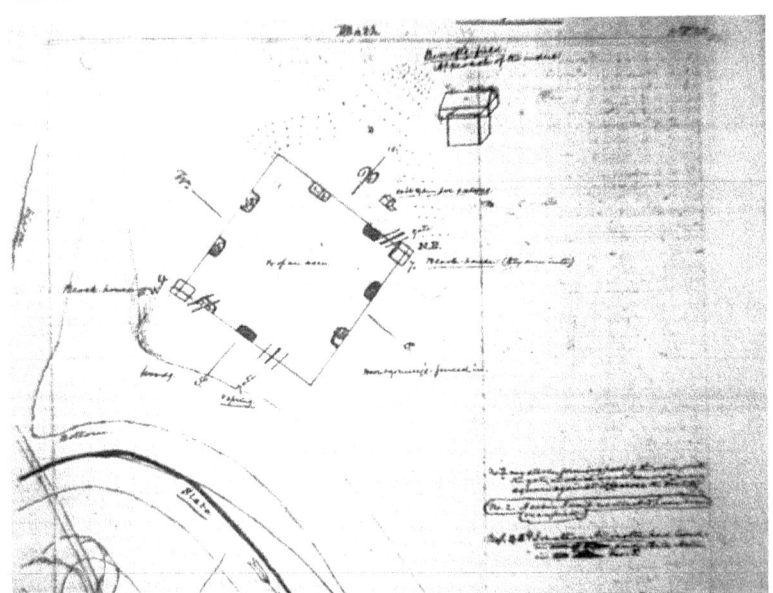

ABOVE: Ravine at Morgan's Station looking southwest from the station site.

BELOW: View of Slate Creek and the ravine (left side of picture) from Morgan's Station.

Site of Enoch Smith's Station about a quarter of a mile on Hinkston Pike from Maysville Road.

or 8 months old) lying tomahawked. It was a very plain case. They had marched her that far in her shift, as was visible from the scratches and marks of a burnt wood they had passed through, and there she had given out". The Indians had walked her the night before too hard, and in the morning she could not walk fast enough to suit them.

The Indians had retraced their steps back to their campground five miles away near the current city of Hope, close to the head of Little Slate Creek. There the Indians gathered their knapsacks and other belongings left behind before the raid, and headed south toward the west fork of Slate Creek which they followed down to the main stream of Slate near the present town of Means. From there they picked up the main trail heading toward the Ohio River. About five miles away they came to Beaver Creek, which they followed downstream until they reached the Licking River. This route roughly follows the course of US 460 to Frenchburg, and Ky 1274 from Frenchburg to Cave Run Lake. "About seven miles on Beaver [Creek] the Indians had turned a little ways down", says Wade, "where they got on to it and massacred a son of Robert Craig's, about 4 or 5 years old. The next were nine – about five miles further. Two of these that were left for dead; the first, Mrs. Robert Craig, died of her wounds seven days later. The other, Betsy Becraft.... recovered entirely". Also killed at the site were Mrs. Craig's infant son, Mrs. Young's son, two children of Mrs. Baker, and three children of Mrs. Becraft. This fork of Beaver Creek was later known as Murder Branch. The site of the tragedy now lies under Cave Run Lake. Betsy Becraft was taken to Lexington and placed under the care of Dr. Richard Downing, and despite a deep depression in her skull three inches in diameter, she fully recovered and remarried. [19]

    Smith's party continued the pursuit, despite the obvious danger in which they were placing the captives. "Twenty-five miles from this the Indians appeared to be gaining on us, and going so fast that Enoch Smith said it was not worthwhile to go any further. The [Indian] horses were well loaded and made a deep track as they stamped in the ground". But the Indians started to lighten their load, dropping packs and other items in order to move more quickly. They were outpacing their pursuers. "We understood afterwards from those who returned that before the last massacre five Indians had slipped off to one side, each with a female prisoner, with an arrangement to meet again in 2 or 3 days on Little Sandy. By this ingenious measure they both evaded pursuit and the necessity of making a flight more rapid than the prisoners were capable of making. (Those women were Clarinda Allington, Alexander Baker's wife and daughter, Rachel Becraft, and Joe Young's wife). The women were kept on Little Sandy for 32 days before being carried over the Ohio.... Besides this, there was only one prisoner, a white boy about fourteen years of age, Ben, a son of Abraham Becraft, was left with the Indians. They carried him with themselves on a horse, and took him almost directly to Detroit, scarcely stopping at their towns. There they sold him to a Scotchman, who put him in a store, gave him a pretty good slight at writing, and made such an improvement on him as you never saw put on anyone. At Wayne's Treaty they had to go and get him and give him up. He came back with no Indian paint, and was nicely dressed. But he soon got to be a Becraft again".

Now the militia decided to stop the pursuit and turned back. The site of the massacre and the speed at which the Indians were traveling made Smith's decision seem the sensible thing to do. As he was turning back, Enoch Smith dispatched Michael Cassidy to urgently give a report of the events of the past two days to Simon Kenton at his home near Limestone. Kenton had a veteran group of Indian fighters that he used to regularly pursue Indian parties, sometimes following them deep into Ohio. Upon receiving the report, Kenton quickly raised 32 men and began tracking the Indians where they crossed the Ohio River and were following the Scioto River north. Among the men raised were Captain Joshua Baker and his men, Captain Nathaniel Massey and his men, Michael Cassidy

Morgan's Station

from Enoch Smith's party, Joseph Jones, Moses Fowler, Captain James Ward and his men, and among the others were men named Washburn, Whiteman and Ireland.[20]

#

White Wolf and his party, now somewhat fewer in number due to the five that had left the party in Kentucky for the Little Sandy River with the women, and a few who had traveled on to their towns, had moved hard and quickly over the past three days. With only the boy to take along on horseback, they had been able to make good time. Now in the Ohio territory and much closer to home, they stopped close to sunset and made camp at Paint Creek a quarter of a mile upstream from Little Copperas Mountain (three miles east of current Bainbridge, Ohio). They were tired, and after the fires were built, they lay down and fell to sleep soundly. Sutawnee lay near the campfire near her father, White Wolf, and her husband, Stand-in-Water. Sleep would not come to her, and she lay propped up on one elbow staring into the fire. Thinking about how much the Kentucky area had changed, how all hope of driving out the white men was gone, and the successful raid on Morgan's Station. She wondered about her father, and the stories he told her about his childhood, not as White Wolf, but as the white boy John Ward. She thought of Bahd-ler, the ferocious white man who had been condemned to be burned at the stake by the Shawnees when he had been captured, and how she had nursed him back to health from running so many gauntlets so that he could run more at other Shawnee towns. And he survived it all, and managed to escape. One of the camp dogs that had been sleeping next to her suddenly rose, cocked his head and growled softly. Sutawnee patted his head and spoke softly, and the dog settled back to where it had been. She then threw back her blanket and rose. The fire was getting low. She moved to the pile of firewood collected earlier and refueled the little blaze. As new flames blossomed from the wood, the whole camp was thrown into a flickering light, and Sutawnee was silhouetted against the campfire. Sutawnee lay down again and covered herself; sleepiness came upon her at last and she drifted off. The fire continued to burn brightly and the dog that had stood up before aroused again, stretched and ambled over toward the creek. It paused for leg-lifting rituals at two shrubs, then a tree, and then a wafting breeze brought to its nose an alien scent; to its ears now came the faint popping of a twig and its hackles stood erect and it began barking loudly as it ran back to the camp. [21]

#

    At this moment Simon Kenton was silently moving his men into position around the camp. He was thankful for the gurgling of the nearby Paint Creek which overrode the sound of their approach. He had split his men into three groups; Captains Joshua Baker and James Ward and their men had been sent over to the left, Captains Nathaniel Massey and Michael Cassidy and their men to the right, and Kenton and nine others in the center. The plan agreed upon was that no attack was to be made until dawn. When the warriors arose and squatted in a group around the fire, a single fusillade might enable them to wipe out the majority of the Indians at once.

    Captain James Ward watched the silhouetted figure near the fire and carefully brought his rifle to bear. His finger was tightening on the trigger when Moses Fowler suddenly tapped his shoulder and whispered, "Captain, it's a woman"! Ward looked closely and, as the figure turned sideways to him, saw the outline of ample breasts under her buckskin and lowered his rifle, unaware that he had just come within a hairsbreadth of killing his own niece.

    The barking dog had now aroused the Indians, who stood in wonder at what the dog was upset about. The warriors began to mill around the campfire.

    Joshua Baker was an impatient man and one who could not follow orders well. He passed the word to his men to fire on the count of three. James Ward, knowing the majority would aim at the broad chest of the nearest Indian, aimed a head shot, again unaware that the figure at which he was aiming was his own brother, whom he scarcely even remembered.

The explosions came with a frightening unexpectedness. As if a huge hand had slapped him, White Wolf as slammed backwards off his feet and crumpled lifelessly. Instantly the warriors sprang away from the shooting. Stand-in-Water pitched his blanket over the flames – a trick he had learned from the stories of Tecumseh's exploits – and in the darkness snatched Sutawnee's hand and let her to a protected spot. The Indians let go with a volley of wild shots in return, causing the whites to dodge for cover.

Chief Sco-tach gave his braves the word to begin to move to the east toward Paint Creek, where they would mount their horses and ride, taking no risk of trying to save anything except themselves and the horses. The maneuver went well, even though the whites followed them slowly and continued an intermittent shooting. As early dawn began to break, the Indians reached their horses, mounted their horses and thundered off to the northeast. No pursuit by Kenton and his men was attempted.

Returning to the camp, Kenton found that Joseph Jones had been mortally shot through the chest. Simon Kenton was furious at the failure of the attack through the disobedience of Baker and his men. But there was little time to waste. He ordered the little camp plundered and a hasty withdrawal made. Since they had no spade, they tied the body of Jones high in a tree to keep it from being found and mutilated by returning warriors.

Baker's party gathered around the body of the first Shawnee shot and an argument broke out among them as to who had killed him, since, of all the guns that had fired, only one bullet had struck him, and that one directly between the eyes. Fowler claimed loudly that the head-shot had come from his Captain, James Ward. There was doubt. But Ward knew. And no one objected when he unsheathed his knife and bent to remove the scalp. Unknowingly, James Ward had slain and scalped his brother. [22]

###

There is some evidence that there were others present at the station at the time of the attack who did not reside there. At one time James Wade makes mention that Reuben Cofer's horse was at the station at the time of the attack, so it is possible that Cofer was there as well. It is possible that other people from nearby cabins were at Morgan's Station at the time of the attack and probably escaped.

Those of whom there is note that were killed or captured as part of the raid on Morgan's Station include:

Abraham Becraft   Escaped to Pleak's Cabin
    Wife, Rachel + Captured, killed on the trail
    Daughter, Ruth + Killed at the Station
    Daughter, Betsy Captured, left for dead but survived
    Son, Benjamin Captured, released at Wayne's Treaty
    Child +   Captured, killed on the trail
    Child +   Captured, killed on the trail
    Child +   Captured, killed on the trail
    Infant +   Captured, killed on the trail
Harry Martin   Escaped to Montgomery's Station
    Wife, Sarah (Morgan) Escaped to Montgomery's Station
    Son, John Escaped to Montgomery's Station
    Daughter, Elizabeth Escaped to Montgomery's Station
Robert Craig   Escaped
    Wife + Captured, left for dead, later died
    Son + Captured, killed on the trail
    Infant son + Captured, killed on the trail
Joseph Young   Escaped to Anderson's cabin

    Wife, Elizabeth Captured, traded to French on Ohio River, later released
    Son + Captured, killed on the trail
  Alexander Baker + Killed at the Station
    Wife, Susan Captured, released at Wayne's Treaty
    Son, William + Captured, killed on the trail
    Daughter, Nancy Captured, traded to Canadians, and never heard from again
    Daughter, Polly Captured, later rescued from the Cherokees by William Whitley
    Child + Captured, killed on the trail
  Old Mrs. Allington Escaped to Pleak's cabin
  Andrew Duncan Escaped to Anderson's cabin
  James Wade Escaped to Troutman's Station
  Clarinda Allington Captured, living with the Cherokees, not released at Wayne's Treaty, subsequently released
  Abel Morgan Escaped to Boonesborough
  David Douglas Escaped to Boonesborough [23]

  Following the attack on Morgan's Station, several of the outlying settlements were temporarily abandoned. Peter Troutman left his station the same day after James Wade gave him the news of the attack that morning. He loaded his wagon and family and fled to the relative safety of Mount Sterling. James Lane and Enoch Smith moved in to Mount Sterling for a short while. This influx of settlers from the outlying areas added to the growth surge of the new town.[24]

  Late in 1792 President George Washington commissioned General Anthony Wayne, a young veteran of the Revolutionary War, to raise an army, train it, and assemble the army in the area of Cincinnati Ohio. He commenced assembling his army in Pittsburgh. The two previous failed campaigns of Harmer and St. Clair – in which each had been defeated by the Indians under Little Turtle, had given hope to the British of retaining their claims to the Northwest Territory. General Wayne arrived to the Ohio territory in the summer of 1793, awaiting word from Washington to attack. In September, 1793 he received word from Washington to commence the campaign. Wayne established as his headquarters Fort Jefferson, about seventy-five miles north of Cincinnati.

The Indians continued raids into the Kentucky settlements throughout 1793 designed to steal horses and take advantage of individual opportunities. William Sudduth related in Reverend Shane, "In the spring of 1793 the Indians stole a great many horses ….". At one point during this time the Indians had made a large camp in the Red River valley and had collected more than 70 horses.

Sudduth continues with the story of a chief named Blackfish and how he and another Indian one night entered the stables where one settler was keeping a prized stud horse, led him out with the bridle, and rode away over twenty miles. "He stated that he took the horse to Detroit and sold him for a keg of rum and lay drunk on it until it like to have killed him. He also stated that they got seventy horses that trip on the Red River".

Horse theft increased in 1794, and in March of that year James Lane and Samuel Downing led a party of 13 men to the headwaters of the Red River. James Wade had been recruited as their pilot. While asleep in their camp with no sentry posted the party was surprised by the Indians they were looking for, and narrowly escaped with their lives leaving guns and blankets behind. Daniel Clifton was wounded and caught by the Indians in the dark as he tried to make his escape. He was tomahawked. Afraid that the Indians would follow up their success and ambush them on the trail, the men hurriedly distanced themselves from the camp and made their way back home.

In late December Wayne led a group of men north to the area of St. Clair's defeat and built Fort Recovery. The spot of the battle had been easy to find. William Sudduth was part of the group of men who reached Fort Recovery in 1794, and he said, "We encamped on the battle ground which was literally covered with bones of men who had fallen in that battle". Several other men had also joined the campaign in the summer of 1794 from the Montgomery County area, including Joshua Baker, James Wade, Harry Martin, George Harper, Levi Lockhart, John Hanks, Luke Hood (grandfather of General John Bell Hood) and John Crawford. [25] Wayne then continued his march north to within forty miles of the British stronghold Fort Miami, near present Toledo, Ohio and established aptly-named Fort Defiance. There were over 1300 Indians assembled in the area, all expecting support from the British in the upcoming battle.

On August 20, 1794 Wayne's army advanced again and engaged the Indians at Fallen Timbers, just south of Toledo. The battle lasted less than an hour, and the well trained and disciplined army under General Wayne routed the Indians. The Indians fled to Fort Miami, where the British declined to give them protection due to the risk of war with the Americans. After the establishment of Fort Wayne, a peace was negotiated with the Indians at the signing of the treaty at Greenville, Ohio. One of the terms of the treaty was that the Indians were given a short period of time to return all of the captives that they had taken. This for the most part was done. Several of the Morgan's Station captives were returned at this time as a result of the treaty. By 1796 the British were turning over their forts in the Northwest Territory to the Americans.

Ralph Morgan finally moved his family to the site of Morgan's Station in 1794. The Station was not rebuilt. Ralph sold a piece of the land, possibly including the station site itself, to his cousin Andrew Swearingen. James Lane said to Reverend Shane, "Andrew Swearingen built the current house at Morgan's Station". The old stone house was built from locally quarried stone in about 1795 or 1796, and was built with defensive measures in mind. It has stone walls that are two feet thick, and the basement walls are over three feet thick. There is no evidence that Ralph Morgan built the house or ever lived in the stone house. Since it was built, the house has had many different owners. [26]

After the attack on Morgan's Station in 1793, the station slowly declined until nearly all memories were gone. The same can nearly be said for Ralph Morgan. He moved to the site with his family in 1794, but always lived a reclusive lifestyle. His last two daughters, Drusilla (born in 1795) and Sarah (born in 1797), were born and married at Morgan's Station. The two sisters actually married two brothers, William and John McCullough. Drusilla and William were married in 1815, and Sarah and John were married in 1814. Sarah and John had fourteen children in sixteen years. [27] [b]

By 1796 the Indian raids into Kentucky had come to an end. It is said that the raid on Morgan's Station on April 1, 1793, while not the last action taken by Indians against the settlers in Kentucky, was the last significant Indian raid in Kentucky.

Montgomery County and
The War of Rebellion

1860 - 1861

For years before the combat of the Civil War began Kentuckians had sponsored a spirit of compromise on a national level. Men such as Henry Clay, John J. Crittenden and John C. Breckinridge worked tirelessly to find a lasting solution for the differing philosophies of government between the Southern states rights advocates and the Northern federal government advocates. The choice of slavery by the Southern states was considered a crucial issue in the debate over the rights of each state.

Kentucky found itself divided on the issues. It has been said that at this time Kentucky was emotionally part of the South and geographically part of the mid-west. Both Jefferson Davis and Abraham Lincoln were born in Kentucky – Davis in Todd County, and Lincoln in nearby Larue County. The two men were comparable in age and even looked strikingly similar. But politically these two sons of Kentucky pulled the state in opposite directions. Kentucky was one of four border states, including Maryland, Delaware and Missouri. These were all slaveholding states like the South, but politically more aligned with the North. Yet the agricultural economies of the deep South were dependent on slave labor, and anyone opposed to slavery was attacking not only the moral issue, but the much more personal economic issue and the source of wealth for many southerners.

On November 6, 1860 Abraham Lincoln, an avowed abolitionist, was elected President of the United States. This was an affront to many southern states, and was the culmination of the political debates raging over the past few decades indicating that no compromise could be reached. This was the last straw for many southern states. In Montgomery County the news of Lincoln's election was something of a surprise. The official vote total in Kentucky for Lincoln was 1,364 – which seems quite low considering the fact that the Union sympathizers controlled the Legislature after the election. One is tempted to believe that the votes were counted "Breathitt County style". [1]

On December 20, 1860 South Carolina rushed to be the first state to officially vote to secede from the Union. And during this fateful four month period of time between the election in November and the inauguration in March, the Kentucky legislature lacked only a few votes of deciding to join the Confederacy.

On March 4, 1861 Abraham Lincoln was inaugurated in Washington, D.C. as the sixteenth President of the United States. On March 8, 1861 the Confederate Convention held in Montgomery, Alabama adopted a constitution.

With the news of the firing on Fort Sumter in Charleston harbor in South Carolina, all of southern Ohio became extremely agitated. Kentucky was thought to surely secede and go with the south, leaving only the Ohio River to separate Cincinnati from the Confederates. Living in Cincinnati at this time was George McClellan, who had recently retired from the Army with the rank of Captain, and who was now intent on utilizing his tremendous organizational skills in the pursuit of a railroad career. McClellan had graduated from West Point in 1846.

The fact is that Kentucky Governor Beriah Magoffin during the month of April rejected calls to raise an army from both Lincoln (April 15th) and shortly thereafter from Davis. The Kentucky Legislature adopted a resolution of strict neutrality, and actually ordered troops to be raised to prevent the invasion of the state, by either the Union armies or the Confederate armies.

Cincinnati at this time was panic-stricken, especially in light of the fact that Ohio had no state militia and no standing home guard. In fact, it was defenseless. Ohio Governor William Dennison was under siege from the citizens in Cincinnati to do something to provide for protection. George McClellan's name was on the lips of many prominent citizens, fueled by his very public statements that he was not interested in a command position. After playing hard to get and entertaining offers from New York, on April 23, 1861 George McClellan accepted the commission of Major General of the Ohio Militia Volunteers, and set about to immediately establish the militia. His organizational skills were superb and exceptional, and soon order was established out of chaos. [2]

Governor Dennison was so impressed with the results, that he forcefully imposed on Washington to have McClellan appointed a Major General in the regular Army. Three weeks after undertaking his commission in Ohio, McClellan received on May 14, 1861 a commission as a Major General in the regular Army. Cincinnati was now feeling slightly more secure with thousands of troops pouring into the camps. And the camps were now under the control of the regular Army, under George McClellan.

McClellan's primary concern was to secure the neutrality of Kentucky. He began negotiations with Kentucky Governor Beriah Magoffin. The contract was agreed upon in early June at a meeting at the Burnet House in Cincinnati (the same hotel where Lincoln had stopped on February 12, 1861 as he was making his way to Washington for the inauguration) between McClellan and General Simon Bolivar Buckner, who was then the Inspector General of the Kentucky State Guard. The agreement sealed Kentucky's neutrality under the following conditions:

    1) Kentucky protected United States Property within it boundaries;

    2) Kentucky enforced the laws of the United States; and

    3) Kentucky would cause any Confederate forces to be removed from the state, and in the event that they did not, McClellan reserved the right of occupancy to remove the Confederate forces, and then he would withdraw.

In Buckner's report to the Governor dated June 10, 1861 about the agreement, he stated that, "The well-known character of General McClellan is a sufficient guarantee for the fulfillment of every stipulation on his part."

However, Union soldiers began to amass at Cairo, Illinois under Major General Ulysses S. Grant, and along the Illinois and Ohio borders, which caused one Kentucky State Senator to fire-off a letter of protest to Lincoln. Lincoln responded in an apologetic manner, stating that he was not aware that Cairo was in the senator's state boundaries, and that if he (Lincoln) was misinformed he would have the soldiers removed immediately.[3]

Governor Magoffin began to organize a strong State Guard to protect Kentucky's neutrality. For the most part the soldiers seemed to be secessionists, which led the Governor's critics to claim that the State Guard would eventually go to war on the Confederate side. This subsequently proved to be true.

In response, the Union elements in the state began to organize a Home Guard, which eventually would be armed by the Union since nearly all the northern counties in Kentucky were falling under the influence of the Union.

In Montgomery County, lines were being drawn. As long time Montgomery County resident Leeland Hathaway, CSA, stated, "all were forced to take sides. It was hard to look upon our friends and schoolmates and on our kindred by ties of blood with suspicion and to feel that arms in their hands were to drive us into the ranks or to shoot us for disloyalty." [4a]

In 1860, 36.3% of the potential voters in Montgomery County were slaveholders. In Kentucky, there were over 225,000 slaves, which was an average of 2.7 slaves per farm. Dr. John Magarvey Prewitt observed, "As to the division of sympathy in Montgomery County, it is hard to state at this late date (1937), but as veterans of the Confederacy greatly outnumbered the veterans of the Union army, I would have to say our sympathies were strongly southern."

Yet the division in the county was severe, as noted by the Presbyterian Church which split into the Southern Presbyterian Church (which is still standing on Main Street) and the Northern Presbyterian Church which was across the street. The two churches did not reunite until 1939, fully seventy-four years after the war was over.

By the summer of 1861, combat engagements began between the Union and the Confederates. On June 11, George McClellan's Ohio troops repulsed a Confederate force at Rich Mountain, West Virginia. On July 21, the first battle of Bull Run outside of Washington, DC was fought with the Confederates holding their ground and the Union Army retreated north of Washington before they could regroup. On July 27 President Lincoln replaced General Irvin McDowell with General George McClellan as head of the Army of the Potomac. Brigadier General Robert Anderson, of Fort Sumter fame, fills McClellan's command in Cincinnati.

On July 25, 1861 John J. Crittenden, US Senator from Kentucky, in a last-ditch effort to find a compromise with the Southern States, introduces the Crittenden Resolution, calling for the American Civil War to be fought to preserve the Union and not for the abolition of slavery, and the resolution was passed by Congress on the same day.

In August, 1861, Colonel Humphrey Marshall established in Owen County, Kentucky a Confederate camp near Lusby's Mill, on a high hill which commanded an extensive view of the surrounding counties. Hundreds of men assembled there to join the Confederate Army, the majority of whom succeeded in making their way south, while others returned to their homes. [5] Also in Owen County was a second recruiting camp in Vallandingham's Barn near Lusby's Mill. Thus Owen County became known as a hotbed for Confederate recruiting.

A few short months of strained peace existed in Kentucky during the summer of 1861, but this was shattered when on September 3, 1861 General Sydney Albert Johnson marched into Kentucky from Tennessee and subsequently occupied Bowling Green on September 18, 1861. Johnson was born in 1803 near Frankfort, Kentucky in the little town of Washington. A large portion of the State Guard and other volunteers marched south to join Johnson's army. The Union forces now had reason within the treaty with Kentucky to cross the river from Illinois and Ohio, occupying Paducah, Smithland and Feliciana.

A primary road from eastern Kentucky into Virginia was the Pound Gap Road, which extended from Mount Sterling to Hazel Green, Prestonsburg, Pikeville, through the Pound Gap and finally to Lynchburg, Virginia. This road was originally engineered in 1817 from a series of Indian trails, and then served as the principal highway for commerce in the area. With Mount Sterling being the furthest town of any size at the edge of the Bluegrass region, the town soon became the staging area and supply depot for Union operations in eastern Kentucky.

Confederate training camps, generally small operations, were becoming numerous in eastern Kentucky. On October 23, 1861 Union General William "Bull" Nelson with the 2nd Ohio and units of Home Guard Militia, including members of the Montgomery County Home Guard, attacked a Confederate camp at West Liberty and at Hazel Green and dispersed the rebels, chasing them down the Pound Gap Road into Virginia. Five prisoners were sent back to Mount Sterling. After Nelson withdrew from eastern Kentucky, the rebels re-emerged under General Humphrey Marshall [b], and Union loyalists and Home Guardsmen were quite concerned for their safety.

The Home Guard had now taken an active role in confronting Confederate camps and Southern sympathizers. Thomas W. Parsons, who lived on Richmond Avenue in Mount Sterling, kept a diary of his participation in the pro-Union Home Guard unit in Montgomery County which was later published in <u>Incidents & Experiences in the life of Thomas W. Parsons</u>. The Home Guard was beginning to receive arms from the Union and they were undertaking drills in military maneuvers at various camp sites. One time Parsons and a small group of Home Guardsmen waited most of a night alongside a fence near Judy waiting for a Confederate sympathizer who was driving 75 mules at night south to the Confederates. He was captured and the mules confiscated.

On December 4, 1861 the US Senate, in a vote of 36 – 0, expelled John C. Breckenridge of Kentucky because he had joined the Confederate Army. Breckenridge had a distinguished political career, and had served as Vice-President of the United States from 1857 to 1861 under President James Buchanan.

1862

By early February, 1862 Major General Ulysses S. Grant has begun the Mississippi Valley campaign. He marched from Cairo, Illinois up the Tennessee River and into Tennessee. Sydney Johnson's Confederate army in Bowling Green did not confront Grant, but rather fell back into Mississippi protecting the strategic railroad lines. In Tennessee Grant captures Fort Henry on the Tennessee River on February 6th, which was commanded by the former Inspector General of the Kentucky State Guard, Simon Bolivar Buckner. Marching a short distance overland toward the east, Grant captures Fort Donelson on the Cumberland River on February 16th. By the end of February the Confederate troops abandon Nashville to Grant's approaching army.

At the beginning of summer Montgomery County had a strong, well armed Home Guard. On July 15, 1862 John Hunt Morgan and his cavalry are reported in the area of Paris and Cynthiana. Home Guard units from Maysville to Mount Sterling are mustered to Paris. On July 17th Morgan attacks Cynthiana and routes the local forces.

First Action in Montgomery County

Captain George M. Jesse, a native of Owen County in northern Kentucky, had recruited, trained, uniformed and armed a group of 215 men in his home area and they were marching to join the Confederate forces in Virginia. They had planned to take the Pound Gap Road from Mount Sterling into Virginia where they would formally offer their services. A Union cavalry patrol had spotted the rebels as they were passing North Middletown, and dispatched couriers with the news to nearby Union troops. As the rebels continued toward Mount Sterling, passing near Sideview, a "young lady", reportedly the sister of long-time Holt Avenue resident Mrs. Sallie Reppert, rode into town to give the alarm that the rebels were at hand. [6]

At sunrise on the morning of July 29 the new recruits in their fine uniforms and new weapons advanced on Mount Sterling astride their horses down the Maysville Pike led by a whiskered man named Stamper. They were met at the north end of town (at about current Maysville and High Streets) by a few soldiers of the 18th Kentucky Regiment and the assembled Home Guard, including Captain John Evans, Provost Marshall of the Guard, William Voris, and others in front of the Sterling House [7] (which was probably a local hotel or boarding house adjacent to the Court House [8]). Stamper called out to the Home Guard assembled under Captain Evans, brief words were exchanged, and in short order the new recruits were engaged by the Home Guard. At this moment the Union cavalry that had been pursuing the rebels appeared and panic swept the green rebel force, with the rebels jumping from their horses and running into nearby corn fields leaving guns, swords, pistols and everything else that could impede their flight. [9] There were casualties now on the street, wounded and dead on both sides.

The rebels were relentlessly pursued, and the story is told of one youth who was murdered in cold blood while pleading for his life on the west side of Maysville Pike just north of High Street. The rebels attempted to pass through the town, when they were fired upon by the Home Guards who had made a fortress of the Court House and many private residences. While the Home Guard was pouring a galling fire into them from the buildings, the Federals were pressing them from the rear, the result being a running fight which lasted until late in the afternoon. [10 c] Some fled westward by staying off the main roads and managed to get into a skirmish with pursuing Unionists around the school house which was on the Thompson Station Road a short distance south of Sewell Shop near the Clark County line. Clifton Prewitt, grandfather of John Marshall Prewitt, recounted how they were in class that day when the skirmish began and how they crouched under their school benches while bullets whistled around the building.

Thomas Parsons estimated the casualty figures at 3 Union defenders dead; and of the 215 rebels, 13 were killed,13 wounded, and 103 captured on the day of the fight and the following day.

The Confederate invasion of Kentucky
By the summer of 1862 the Confederate government was desperately seeking official recognition as an independent nation from various European countries and to be able to secure sizable supplies from them. In order to earn this recognition, a plan was put forth to invade and hold Union territories in order to show that the Confederacy could actually win the war. By late summer, all of the armies of the Confederacy undertook offensive operations. The second battle of Bull Run was fought on August 30th, and Robert E. Lee advanced the Army of Northern Virginia into Maryland. General Edmund Kirby Smith with 10,000 men marched from Knoxville in coordination with General Braxton Bragg and his 30,000 men who marched from Chattanooga headed for Kentucky and the Ohio River.

General Smith bypassed the Union-held Cumberland Gap, and swiftly entered Kentucky. An inexperienced Union garrison of 6,500 men at Richmond, Kentucky met Smith's force and was completely defeated on August 30, 1862. The next day the Mayor of Lexington surrendered the city, and Smith entered the town on September 1st. The swiftness of Smith's army caused great alarm for the Unionist and the Home Guardsmen, who reorganized and marched to Maysville to make a stand at the Ohio River. [11]

Continuing his march westward, with apparent complete disregard for Bragg's location, Smith marched his troops into Frankfort and Harrodsburg. Smith then turned back east with a portion of his forces and marched to Mount Sterling to cut off the escape of the Union defenders stationed at the Cumberland Gap. By mid-September Mount Sterling was occupied by units of General Humphrey Marshall's command. Earlier units, including the unit under Captain Peter Everett, entered Mount Sterling by September 5. [12] General Edmund Kirby Smith was the highest ranking officer to come to Mount Sterling, arriving on September 29, 1862. The starving Union army from the Cumberland Gap made its way to West Liberty, and then to Greenup – a feat said to be one of the most difficult marches in the war. General Smith's army reached as far north as Fort Mitchell and Erlanger. Maysville was occupied during the week of September 15, 1862 by Major John Holliday.

The Confederate commanders were expecting that this swift and early success in Kentucky would bring thousands of new recruits and volunteers into the ranks of the invading armies. The minimum objective was to keep the army at the same fighting level despite losses from battles and camp sickness.

Now General John Hunt Morgan began his march through Kentucky, which caused a great deal more alarm than the advance of Humphrey Marshall through eastern Kentucky. The following telegraph between Union commanders is dated September 24, 1862:

> Brigadier General Henry Heth
> Commanding
> Georgetown, Kentucky
> GENERAL:

General Morgan crossed the Kentucky River at Proctor last night. He is moving on Mount Sterling. Push on to intercept him, marching at night if necessary. [13]

At this time in Mount Sterling, General Humphrey Marshall had set up the command of his 5,000 man Army of Eastern Kentucky in the town and had begun vigorously recruiting. At the height of the Confederate offensive success in Kentucky he made a speech to his recruits, the Fourth Kentucky Cavalry, which, in the light of subsequent events, proved to be prophetic. He assured them that his personal knowledge of the men running the political machinery of the Federal government, and his acquaintance with their prominent military men, who had been his classmates at West Point and his comrades in Mexico, led him to believe that they would not easily be defeated in their relentless crusade against the Southland. He was aware that the new recruits were mere boys, who entertained the idea that they were out on a "frolicsome kind of high roller," and that it would require but a brief time to roll back the masses of invading Northmen, *a la* Manassas. He said that they must at once unload their minds of such "foolish notions," and prepare to endure a long siege and to see grim-visaged war in all its horrors. He stripped the war picture of all gilt and fancy tints, leaving in view nothing but a dark, forbidding perspective. [14]

General Braxton Bragg's army marched out of Chattanooga into Kentucky and was shadowed by General Don Carlos Buell's army that was in Nashville. Bragg attacked and defeated the Union garrison at Munfordville, Kentucky on September 14. The Confederates were now clearly in command of the central portion of Kentucky. Buell raced his army around Bragg all the way to Louisville before turning around to face him. Bragg's army continued marching toward the Ohio, and passing through Frankfort installed a provisional Confederate governor. The fall was exceedingly hot and dry in Kentucky. Looking for water, Bragg turned his army westward from Frankfort and collided with Buell's army coming from Louisville. One of the bloodiest battles fought in the civil war was between these two armies at Perryville (outside of Frankfort, Kentucky) on October 8, 1862. After the battle the Confederate armies could not hold the ground that they had captured. The lack of new recruits greatly frustrated Bragg. On September 25th he wrote from Bardstown, Kentucky to the Adjutant-General Confederate States Army in Richmond, Virginia, "I regret to say we are sadly disappointed at the want of action by our friends in Kentucky. We have so far received no accession to this army. General Smith has secured about a brigade – not half our losses by casualties of different kinds. We have 15,000 stand of arms and no one to use them. Unless a change occurs soon we must abandon the garden spot of Kentucky to its cupidity." He went on to say, " ... but at least 50,000 men will be necessary, and a few weeks will decide the question." [15] Thirteen days later the question was decided at Perryville.

On September 22, 1862 Northern newspapers published Lincoln's Emancipation Proclamation, issued three days after Robert E. Lee was defeated at the battle of Antietam, Maryland and withdrew back to Virginia.

The Confederate invasion of the North had hit its high water mark by the end of September, and the battle of Perryville was the nail in the coffin. From this point forward, with the exception of Lee's invasion of Pennsylvania a year later which culminated in his defeat at Gettysburg, the Confederacy would be fighting a defensive war with dwindling supplies and troops.

As the invasion began to be pushed back, the Home Guard began their march from Maysville to return to Mount Sterling under Captain Samuel McKee reaching Flemingsburg the first night. Having no tents, they camped out under the stars where ever they could find shelter. The next day they reached Sharpsburg, where they received the news that General Marshall's army of about 5,000 was camped near Jeffersonville on Slate Creek. Being greatly outnumbered, they "did not think it politic to press his rear too hard," so they went into camp at Sharpsburg. By midnight four deserters from Marshall's army stumbled into the pickets posted about a mile out and were interrogated by Judge Richard Apperson. The next day they reached Mount Sterling, and the mounted men dashed in and picked up some of Marshall's stragglers. Later a strong party was sent out the Jeffersonville, or Ticktown, pike and they brought in several prisoners. That night a report reached them that John Hunt Morgan had made a dash to the rear of the Federal army at Lexington, and it was thought that he would

Pound Gap Road from Mount Sterling to Hazel Green to Pikeville.

General E. Kirby Smith
Led Confederate army from
Knoxville during invasion of
Kentucky

General Braxton Bragg
Led larger Confederate army
from Chattanooga during invasion
of Kentucky. Defeated at Perryville.

General Simon Bolivar Buckner
Negotiated Kentucky's neutrality
with General George B. McClellan

Kentucky Governor Beriah Magoffin.
Refused to order troops to either the
Union or Confederate causes.

General George Stoneman.
Graduated West Point in 1846.
Participated in campaign of Atlanta.
Became Governor of California in 1883.

General Don Carlos Buell.
Defeated Braxton Bragg at the battle
of Perryville, ending the Confederate
invasion of Kentucky.

General Stephen G. Burbridge.
Launched attack on Saltville in 1864
from Mount Sterling, where wounded
Union Negro troops were massacred
by the Confederate soldiers.

General George B. McClellan.
Negotiated Kentucky's neutrality with
Simon Boliver Buckner. Later Com-
mander-in-Chief of Union forces.

Colonel Henry L. Giltner.
Fourth Kentucky Cabalry.

Thomas W. Parsons
Served in pro-Union Montgomery County
Home Guard during the Civil War

Site of Bosworth & Drake's Woolen Mill at the
corner of Sycamore and Main in Mount Sterling

Site where Morgan's Third Brigarde
was camped on the night of June 8
and attacked by General Burbridge.

General John Hunt Morgan. Led raid on Mount Sterling in 1864.

Brig. Gen. Basil W. Duke. Brother-in-law of John Hunt Morgan. Second in command of Morgan's cavalry.

Dr. Edward O. Guerrant Kept extensive detailed diaries during the Civil War. Participated in the 1864 raid on Mount Sterling.

Major Leeland Hathaway. Born and raised at "Deer Park" on the Maysville Pike in Mount Sterling.

General John Bell Hood.
Raised on a farm in Montgomery
County on the Winchester Pike.

From this farm John Bell Hood left in 1849 to attend West Point.

John C. Breckinridge. As Vice President of the United States under James Buchanan (above left), and pictured as a Major General in the Confederate Army in 1862 (above right). Related to several distinguished Montgomery County families.

Site of Confederate mass burial grave located at 329 West Main St., Mount Sterling, Ky

Pictured is what remained of the Mount Sterling Court House after Captain Pete Everett's December, 1863 raid when he burned the building to prevent it from being used again as a Federal fortress.

be driven out toward Mount Sterling. So once more the Home Guard took to the road toward Maysville with twenty-five prisoners. Continued rumors of rebels all around them caused the Guard to halt outside of Sharpsburg and go into camp. The next day they then marched the prisoners over to Paris and turned them over to the Federal authorities, and were accompanied back to Mount Sterling by the 22nd Michigan Infantry Regiment and three companies from the 10th Kentucky cavalry. [16]

Under Captain Samuel McKee, who had been appointed Provost Marshall, the Home Guard was mustered out to Chenault's spring two miles south of Mount Sterling to camp in the open air. The command had no tents for the men. It was then, as Parsons recalled, "that the October snow fell, so well remembered by all the soldiers who were in the services in this latitude at that time." (Five inches of snow was recorded in nearby Winchester, Kentucky). Mosgrove recalled that on October 26, 1862 during the retreat from Kentucky, the new Confederate recruits from Mount Sterling struck their first really rough experience, when they encountered the heavy snowstorm high on a mountain on a narrow winding road where some wagons had to be abandoned. Thus began the intensely cold winter of 1862 / 63.

Parsons went on to relate that only later were tents, horses, saddles, blankets, provisions, wagons and other necessities furnished to the Montgomery County Home Guard, and to the other units stationed there at the camp. The camp was called Camp Dooley. [d]

For the next several months Camp Dooley was involved in scouting in the mountains for rebels. Prisoners were continually being brought in. The men scouted as far out as Moorehead, West Liberty, Hazel Green and Stanton. Over this period of time the camp was credited with over 1,400 prisoners turned over to the Provost Marshall in Lexington, Kentucky. Two other battalions were stationed at Irvine and covered from the Kentucky River over to Perry County. [17]

On December 10, 1862 the U.S. House of Representatives passed a bill creating the state of West Virginia.

On Christmas Day a courier came to Mount Sterling from Stanton, twenty miles away, saying that Weed Gay, a notorious guerila of Powell County had made a raid on Stanton that morning, looted some Union citizens, and soldiers were needed to apprehend him. Major Stivers called out sixty men and going at their head went in pursuit. They reached Stanton after dark, pushed up the Red River, and at daylight came up with Weed Gay at the house of John Wills. Gay and twenty-two of his men had been dancing with some of the mountain belles the evening before. Stivers closed in on them and captured Gay and ten others who were in the house. [18] Reports indicate that although Stivers was outnumbered, the swiftness and surprise of the attack completely routed the guerila force. The prisoners were brought back to Camp Dooley.

1863

On the 14th of February, 1863 a small brigade of Kentucky CSA cavalry assembled at McMinnville, Tennessee. Seven hundred and fifty men constituted the organization. The 8th Kentucky CSA cavalry, of which Roy S. Cluke [e] was colonel, Major Robert S. Bullock commanding, was to form the basis of the men to be used in an expedition into Central Kentucky. Colonel Cluke was allowed a couple of brass cannon, howitzers, affectionately called by Morgan's men the "bull pups". They never did very great damage, but they made a lot of noise. They looked to an enemy much bigger than they were. General Morgan furnished his two brothers as part of the staff. The best possible material was designated for this service. The men chosen for the raid were thoroughly acquainted with most of the territory through which Colonel Cluke would have to pass. On the morning that they marched from McMinnville, one hundred rounds of ammunition were counted out and six days rations were issued to each man. The weather was extremely inclement and extraordinarily cold. Hardly had the line been formed until sleet and rain and snow came violently down.[19]

On the 19th of February the little army reached Somerset, Kentucky. A strong Federal force stationed there was alarmed by reports of an army of Confederates approaching from Knoxville, and they hurriedly retreated to Danville, forty-five miles away. In their haste, the Federals neglected to destroy their stores at Somerset. Upon his arrival, Cluke found clear roads and a gracious windfall of stores for his men.[20] In mid-February Camp Dooley was moved out on the Jeffersonville Pike onto the farm of William Tipton about one and a quarter miles from town. There were 4 or 5 inches of snow on the ground. On February 22nd, while on the road marching a prisoner to the Provost Marshall in Lexington, Parsons and another Union guard were warned by Mr. John A. Thompson that Colonel Roy Cluke with some 2000 men was in Winchester where they had just captured the Union command there. Reversing course, they immediately returned to camp and reported to Major Williams. The whole command was then ordered to go out two miles to Congleton's Hill (at Reid Village). Soon thereafter a squad returned with some captured Confederate pickets that had been posted five miles east of Winchester. At sundown orders were received to destroy all stores that could not be transported and to fall back to Paris. A hasty evacuation of the camp ensued, and eighteen wagons were on the Maysville Pike by the end of the day. Cluke had dispatched sixty men under Lt. Colonel Robert G. Stoner, and they followed on and captured all the wagons except two and burned them. One particular team of horses and a wagon were abandoned by their driver, but the team continued on arriving in Paris the next morning. For their loyalty and service, the team was granted a temporary furlough. [21]

By the ninth day of the march Cluke was well into central Kentucky, and had completely mystified and alarmed the Federal commands with nearly no losses of his own. Detachments were sent in every direction to increase the terror of the Federal forces in Lexington, Mount Sterling and

Paris. So smooth had been the operation, that Cluke granted temporary furloughs to the men who lived in the immediate vicinity of Lexington, Mount Sterling, Winchester and Richmond. Only the complete demoralization of his foes would justify Cluke's risking such a measure. By the 24th of February Cluke had concentrated his command at Mount Sterling under Captain Pete Everett [9] and Captain Robert G. Stoner, who established headquarters in the building on the southwest corner of Main and Maysville streets, and the whole day was spent on collecting and distributing horses, equipment and arms. [22]

    By this time the Federals had become somewhat inquisitive and doubtful about the strength of the invaders. The ten thousand infantry did not show up at the Cumberland Gap, and it began to appear that the detachment that was giving them so much trouble was not a very great army after all. Colonel Benjamin P. Runkle had been pursuing Cluke's force since crossing the Kentucky River – seeming to be no more than a day behind them at any time. In Runkle's report written from Mount Sterling on March 5th to Brigadier General Q.A. Gilmore in Lexington, he stated that, "At daybreak on the 25th, I moved forward to Mount Sterling. About two miles from Mount Sterling I met citizens who informed me that the enemy were retreating, and that the rear guard had just passed within one mile of Mount Sterling". A more vivid account comes from Bennett H. Young, who wrote, "A Federal cavalry brigade made a dash at Mount Sterling, Cluke's headquarters. Only two hundred men of the command were at hand at that particular moment. Furloughs had decimated Cluke's forces and they were glad to get out of the town, but they were gladder still that the Federals did not pursue them". The Confederate forces put up a mild resistance, and rang the bells in town to sound the alarm. Young continued saying that, "four hundred of Cluke's furloughed men hastened to the relief of their retreating companions. The Federal cavalry established itself in Mount Sterling but left Colonel Cluke in command of the surrounding country".

The Home Guard unit returned to Mount Sterling from Paris to find that Colonel Runkle had chased the Confederates out of town that morning. Again without tents, the Home Guard went into camp with Runkle's men on the edge of town. One of their men, T.J. Rickets, was very sick and taken to the house of Richard Apperson Jr where he died a few days later. [23]

Cluke's men had moved off above Jeffersonville and camped on Slate Creek. The following day, on the 26th, the entire Federal force marched out to Jeffersonville to "get up a row with Cluke," but Cluke declined the invitation for the fight and moved off toward Owingsville.

Soon thereafter an enterprising and shrewd Confederate spy dressed in a Federal uniform, entered the headquarters of the Union commander in Mount Sterling and managed to pocket some blank printed forms. Returning to the Confederate lines with the forms, one of them was filled in as an order purporting to be from the commander at Lexington, directing the commander at Mount Sterling to march immediately to Paris, twenty miles north of Lexington, to repel an impending Confederate raid. Confederate scout Clark Lyle, dressed in full Union uniform, rode into Mount Sterling at top speed, lashing his horse at every step. He rushed to the headquarters of Colonel Runkle, and delivered the orders. The bugles were instantly sounded, and the Federal cavalry brigade moved out to Paris. Hardly had the sound of the jingling sabers ceased along the gravel road which led from Mount Sterling to Paris, before Cluke with his reorganized force re-entered the town and captured the garrison and the stores. [24]

Colonel Runkle's report to General Gilmore states, "On arriving at Paris on the morning of the 27th, I found the reported advance of the rebels was a false alarm. I halted to rest my men and horses, and to await orders from the general commanding. I received an order to pursue Cluke and use him up. I proceeded to carry out this order. I took every precaution to cut off communication between Paris and Mount Sterling, and sent Lt. Trimble Williams, a brave and gallant soldier, to Mount Sterling. He went into the town among the rebels, and gained all the information I desired, and reported to me on the following morning". Runkle split his command, one traveling toward Mount Sterling on the Paris Pike, and the other via the Winchester Pike. Upon false reports that the rebels were moving against Winchester, Runkle was then ordered to occupy Winchester, which he did and remained until the morning of March 2nd, resting his men and horses.

On March 2nd Runkle drove Cluke out of Mount Sterling, across the Slate Creek and into the mountains of Eastern Kentucky. Cluke then received a report that General Humphrey Marshall with 3,000 men was advancing into Kentucky, and Cluke fell back to Hazel Green in Wolfe County, thirty-five miles from Mount Sterling. After a few days at Hazel Green, an epidemic, described as a cross between erysipelas and measles, appeared and half of Cluke's small command was disabled with this dangerous malady.

Meanwhile, Cluke sent Colonel Stoner back to Montgomery County just to let the Federals know that he and his men were still around.

On March 14th two Federal expeditions were moved against Cluke at Hazel Green – one under Colonel Walker from Mount Sterling, and the other under Lt. Colonel Wilson from Richmond, aggregating some 1,000 men. As they marched toward Hazel Green, Cluke slipped off to Salyersville. By March 19th Cluke found himself surrounded by the Federal Forces, with strong units on the four points of the compass. His position appeared hopeless to everyone but Cluke, who later reported that, "I surprised them by making my appearance where I was not suspected." Colonel Walker sent a dispatch on the 19th claiming that the rebels were completely hemmed-in, and that they had no other chance of getting out unless by way of Lexington. This dispatch was delivered to headquarters through Captain William D. Ratliff, Tenth Kentucky Cavalry, commanding Colonel Walker's ineffectives left in Mount Sterling. [25]

At this point Cluke's command consisted of only 500 effectives, all the others not fully recovered from the attack of the disease. The only thing Cluke could do was to attack the enemy where he was least expecting it. He was sixty miles from Mount Sterling, and the roads were impassible due to the heavy rains. Cluke resolved to attack Mount Sterling again, and the combination of rain, cold, and slush created by the tramp of the troops rendered the conditions surrounding this march almost unbearable. Before leaving his sick men, Cluke scattered them out into the mountains. Colonel Cluke made a fierce and hard drive at Mount Sterling, and on the morning of the 21st of March appeared before the town and demanded its surrender. This was firmly declined, and the Federal garrison was driven back into the Court House. [26] As Parsons related, "We had only four hundred, dismounted, sick and teamsters under Captain Ratliff of the 10th Kentucky Cavalry and Captain McKee. We were posted in the buildings with bonfires in the streets (to provided sufficient light for the Union marksmen), expecting them to charge the town, but they did not. We could hear an occasional shot some times in one direction and then in another, but as soon as day began to break the shots came faster, and seeing they were gaining nothing they began to burn the town. The first building fired was Drake and Bosworth's Woolen Mill on the [northeast] corner of Main and Sycamore streets, some distance from where any troops were stationed. I have learned since that this was done by one Captain Gentry who owed some personal illwill to Drake. The next house east from the corner on Main, occupied by Rebel sympathizers was passed [this house was occupied by W.T. Howe], and a block further east was fired, and then the Christian Church [on the northeast corner of Main and Bank streets] – the church had always officially promoted emancipation for the slaves - by pouring the oil out of the lamp on the Bible for a starter. An attempt was made to put out this fire but was not successful, the party being fired on by some Rebels concealed in a house across Main Street. The fire communicated to our hospital on the corner of Main and Broadway, but our sick were all gotten out. It then burned on up north along Broadway till it stopped at an open space. I was in that row near the corner and was the last man to leave the room where I was posted." [27] The home of the Postmaster was burned, along with other buildings in the area, in spite of his vehement claims to being a Confederate sympathizer. He could not explain away his Yankee paycheck. [28] The east side and the north side of Mount Sterling were also occupied. The east side of Maysville Street, then known as Dr. Hannah's orchard (encompassing the area from the old Mount Sterling High School south) was alive with Confederates firing at the town, especially the Courthouse. [29] The Union forces then were fortified in the Courthouse, but the citizens of the town prevailed on Captain Ratliff to surrender in order to save the town from complete destruction. The action had lasted an estimated seven hours.

Colonel Cluke filed the following report on March 24th, 1863 from Rockville, Rowan County: "I then moved my command to Mount Sterling, which place I reached about daylight the next morning, where I found the enemy quartered in the Court House and adjoining buildings. I immediately demanded a surrender of the place, which request they refused to comply with. I then gave them twenty minutes to get the women and children from town. That they refused to do also, and fired upon the flag of truce from the Court House and several other buildings immediately around the Court House. My artillery, not coming up in time, I was compelled to fire the town to dislodge the enemy. After several houses had been burned, they surrendered the place; but before surrendering, they kept a continual firing from the buildings upon my men, who were protected by fences, stables and outbuildings around the town. I paroled two hundred eighty-seven privates (14th Kentucky cavalry) and fourteen officers. I paroled them to report to you within thirty days, which I herewith send you. The property destroyed, belonging to the enemy, will reach I think five hundred thousand dollars. I occupied the town about six hours when my scouts reported a large force advancing from Winchester. I immediately moved in the direction of Owingsville. I had not proceeded more than five miles when they made their appearance some two miles in my rear, numbering about twenty-five hundred men, with several pieces of artillery. They would not advance upon me and I quietly advanced on to Owingsville, without pursuit, and from thence on to the above place."[30]

Thomas Parsons was among the prisoners taken at the surrender of the town. They were marched out of town a short distance and about to be paroled, but ordered to fall in again when it was heard that Colonel Israel Garrard of the Seventh Ohio Cavalry was marching from Winchester to the relief of Mount Sterling. Along the route to Owingsville men were paroled, the last of which was Captain McKee's Company D which was paroled at the edge of Owingsville in the yard of Judge Newton Reid. McKee, however, was taken to Richmond and laid in Libby Prison for 13 months. [*In the terms of parole common to both armies, Parsons and the others had sworn to remain neutral. Had they broken the parole without first being duly exchanged for an equal number of parolees or prisoners, they might have well faced the death penalty if recaptured by the Confederate forces. There were, however, many abuses of the vast and loose-knit exchange system on both sides*].

It appeared that a scapegoat was needed for the daring raid of Cluke back to Mount Sterling. So, for his part in the surrender that saved the rest of the town, on March 27th Captain Ratliff was brought up on charges. "For his disgraceful surrender of Mount Sterling, is, subject to the approval of the President, dishonorably dismissed from the military service of the United States". The official inquiry was made, and in the finding dated April 30, 1863 stated "Captain Ratliff, having been honorably acquitted, by the Court of Inquiry, from the charges preferred against him for his surrender of Mount Sterling, he is cleared from all imputations upon his character as a soldier, and will report for duty to the commanding officer of his regiment...."[31]

The battle of Gettysburg, Pennsylvania was fought July 1 – 3, 1863. This marked the last major invasion of the North by the South, and is seen as the turning-point of the War.

On July 4, 1863 the siege of Vicksburg ended with the unconditional surrender of the Confederate defenders to Ulysses S. Grant.

In September of 1863 six men from the mountains of eastern Kentucky were on their way to join the Federal army when they were captured by Frank Ferguson and his desperate gang in Jeffersonville. This group of southern sympathizers had been looting and harassing Federal supporters for quite some time, and their lawlessness required a response. Under the pretext of paroling the six men, Ferguson had them line up, and then shot them all. One man survived – a Mr. Little, who was nursed back to health, and when his tale of Ferguson's dishonorable conduct reached the Federal garrison in Mount Sterling, they mounted up in the first days of October and burned Jeffersonville, or Ticktown as it was then known, to the ground and killed a man named Greenwade who was charged with harboring desperados. Jeffersonville had long been openly hostile to the Federals and had harbored Confederate soldiers since the beginning of the war. [32]

On the night of December 1, 1863 Captain Pete Everett made a dash into Mount Sterling from the east side of town with about 200 Confederate cavalry. The Indiana regiment was camped on the Jeffersonville Pike a short distance from town. Everett's men set fire to the Courthouse and the jail, and broke into the Quartermaster's Department and took what they wanted and left. The Courthouse was destroyed with all its contents, records and all, except for the Deed Books which County Judge Calvin Brock saved at great personal risk. The jail was saved by some of the citizens who help put out the fire. The Indiana Regiment chased Everett to Carrington's three miles beyond Olympia Springs, but never caught him. [33] One can only imagine how desolate the little town of Mount Sterling appeared in the cold gray winter days, having not yet recovered from the burning administered in March of the same year by Cluke in which several blocks of the town were destroyed, only to have the Courthouse burned to the ground. On the other hand, the Courthouse would not serve again as a fortress from which the Federals and the Home Guard could fire upon the Confederate forces.

The Federals then reinforced Mount Sterling beyond its ability to provide food and forage. On the first of January, 1864 the 45th Kentucky under Colonel John Mason Brown moved up from Paris. The march was made during such bitter cold weather that many men received medical attention for frostbit hands and toes. In February General Sturgis came to Mount Sterling with about 5000 cavalry to rest up and recruit, where they remained for about a month.

1864

In March of 1864 General Sturgis' force was ordered south, and a relative tranquility fell over the decimated little town of Mount Sterling. [34] This large force of Union cavalry had strained the already limited and depleted agricultural resources of the county. To some extent the local citizens were glad to see General Sturgis leave.

By mid-April there was Confederate activity along the Pound Gap road. Federal troops were ordered up from Lexington to Mount Sterling with the intent of taking the Pound Gap road toward West Liberty and Paintsville. Again, more Federal forces entered the town and had to bring their own food and supplies to feed the troops. At about this same time plans were being formed for the Federals to march down the Pound Gap Road all the way to Saltville, Virginia to destroy the much needed source of salt for the Confederate armies. By late May the Federal forces headed by General Burbridge departed Mount Sterling headed for their objective at Saltville, Virginia. According to Parsons, this left nearly no Federal troops in Mount Sterling except Captain Edward Barlow's company of 40th Kentucky which was acting a Provost Marshall, and a few men of other regiments left as guards over the property of their regiments.

The Confederate activity along the Pound Gap Road was a prelude to another push by General John Hunt Morgan into Kentucky. As Mosgrove relates the advance of Morgan's Confederate cavalry, "In passing through the gap in the mountains, separating Virginia from Kentucky, we brushed away a small force of Federals, on duty there, and proceeded on a necessarily slow and wearisome march toward Mount Sterling, our first objective point. To better understand subsequent events I must state that the Federal general, Burbridge, with a strong force was at that very time en route to Virginia, his objective point being probably the Saltworks. He was marching on another road, however, nearly parallel with our route. I am unaware that either commander was advised of the contemplated movements of the other. Be that as it may we marched uninterruptedly to Mount Sterling, reaching that place June, 8, 1864. When within about twelve miles of Mount Sterling, about midnight, we left the State Road, turning to the right, and followed a by-path through a woodland as dark as Erebus. We knew that there was a Federal force in or near the town, and General Morgan, who nearly always, sometimes to his sorrow, went right at any obstruction in his front, was anxious to attack the enemy without any unnecessary delay. It would not do, however, to "run in to them" in the dark, especially as we were not certain of their location." He continued, "General Morgan, at daylight, quietly led the column forward, across the farm of Mack Everett, a brother of the noted Confederate free-lance, Captain Pete Everett." Passing near Mack Everett's house, he indicated to Morgan the location of the two Federal camps. Morgan ordered the escape routes out of town blocked, and then began the attack. "And when we charged, Major Holiday, with Clay's battalion, made short work with the smaller one, on our right, which had opened a spirited fire on us. He captured most of them, probably seventy-five or one hundred. The camp between us and the town was more stubbornly defended by two hundred or more men. They were first attacked by Colonel Trimble, who fought them gallantly until reinforced by a battalion of the Second Brigade, there being but three battalions of Giltner's brigade present. The enemy were driven quickly into the town, where the Fourth Kentucky, dismounted, charged them. They poured a galling fire into our ranks from the houses in which they had taken refuge. Captain Swango, of the Tenth Kentucky Mounted Rifles, was killed by a shot from Doctor Drake's house [h], and Captain Moore, of the same battalion, was killed by a shot from a house near the bank." Reflecting on Mount Sterling, Mosgrove added, "this was the third time the town of Mount Sterling had been converted into a fortress and Confederates shot down from the houses. It was probably the meanest town to the Confederate soldier in the State". He went on to say, "The capture was complete by 6 A.M., and Giltner's brigade, or a part of it, took possession of the enemy's tents. The Federals lost about ten killed, the usual proportion of wounded, and about two hundred and seventy-one prisoners. We captured also the camp equipage of Burbridge's absent troopers, consisting of tents, quartermaster and commissary stores and a lot of broken down cavalry horses".[i] Mosgrove goes on, "The capture was a veritable bonanza for our boys, who, being ravenously hungry, immediately and without ceremony sat themselves down to the banquet prepared by the Federals". He described the looting of the Federal soldiers' boots, coats, dress shirts, jackets, pants, etc. A portion of Morgan's men were dismounted, carrying saddles in hopes of capturing a fresh mount along the way. This slowed the progress of the entire group.

General Burbridge had been alerted of Morgan's charge, and was retracing his march, moving up behind them swiftly. Mosgrove acknowledges that the Confederates should have continued out of Mount Sterling, but states that "all the while we were lying supinely on our backs that day and night at Mount Sterling". Meanwhile, General Morgan had dispersed his cavalry toward Lexington, Paris, Cynthiana, Maysville, and Frankfort to raid and harass the Federals there. [j]

Parsons noted that, "the stores were looted, and the Farmer's Bank was robbed of some 90,000 dollars, and the owners of good horses were despoiled of them". This robbery did not go unnoticed by the Confederate authorities. A Judge Advocate charged that "on or about the 8th of June, at or near Mount Sterling, Kentucky after the capture of said town ... Brig John Hunt Morgan commanding, ordered the said Surgeon. R.R. Goode, then serving on his staff, to enter the Farmer's Bank of Kentucky ... and seize the public funds ... for the use of the Confederate States, whereupon said Good took from said bank about $72,000, and failing to account for the same, applied said money to his own use".

There was another bank in Mount Sterling, that of Barnes, White & Co, William Hoffman cashier. As soon as Hoffman learned what was up with the Confederate looting he gathered all the money and slipped out of town in the direction of Lexington, and out of town a few miles the Lexington stage out from Mount Sterling with a lady passenger, overtook him and he boarded it. Along the route Morgan's advance, on the way to Lexington, overtook the stage and as the road men say, "went through it." Hoffman handed the tine box containing the money to the lady and she held it in her hand, and when asked what it contained she said some cheap trinkets she was taking home to her children, and he let her pass at that, and thus saved the Bank. Parsons related that "I was on the street when Mr. Hoffman returned home a few days later and heard him tell how it happened and being a profane man he used words not set down in the Sunday school books."

Morgan was not able to take Lexington by surprise, and was repulsed there. Morgan also had quite a number of men still afoot, and the remaining men in Mount Sterling went into camp on the night of the 8th about a mile out on the Jeffersonville Pike near the tollgate. No one suspected that General Burbridge would ride 90 miles from Prestonsburg in

24 hours and enter straight into battle at daybreak on the morning of June 9, 1864. [35]

The Third Brigade was camped on the hill south of town, at where is now the Montgomery County High School. As Mosgrove related the story, "At the dawning of daylight, June 9th, the enemy, unannounced, charged into our camp. The morning was rainy and somewhat stormy. My own experience was similar to that of others. I was sleeping soundly and did not hear "war's alarm" until Campbell Ross, of the Fourth Kentucky, hurriedly passing my tent called to me, saying the camp was full of Yankees. Poor fellow! He was killed shortly afterward. The bullets were whizzing through my tent, and sooner that I can tell it, I was on my horse, riding like the wind toward a line being formed by Colonel Pryor, who was galloping hither and thither, his clarion voice giving sharp, decisive commands. The charging enemy, only a few rods distant, kept up such a lively fusillade that I was admonished to lie flat down on my horse, in that way hoping to escape to Colonel Pryor's line. A number of the boys had already been captured, some of them before being able to mount their horses. Nearly all of us lost our "baggage", which, however, did not amount to much". The Union also attacked the camp of the First Brigade, under the command of Henry L. Giltner, a native of Sharpsburg, Kentucky. His account stated that the Union forces were "delivering heavy fire from the pike and camp near Mrs. Tipton's and the high hill (Smithville hill) back of the graveyard, next to town." Slowly the Confederates formed their lines and moved to hook up with other camps that were on the road to Lexington. The brigade then moved around [and through] the town to form a junction with Colonel Martin who was on the Lexington Pike. Martin planned to move his Third Brigade to the right along the Ticktown Pike and try to flank the Federals who had now formed up between them and the town. The Third Brigade retreated north around town, crossing the Maysville Pike near the old Grubbs house, and regrouping at the far west end of what is now Winn Street. [36] By 9 A.M. the Confederates began to move against Burbridge's men. They formed a dismounted skirmish line on both side of the Winchester Pike. The Confederates advanced to the Robert Barnes house on Richmond Avenue and there pushed the Federals back to the Apperson house [on the south end of the current viaduct bridge]. The Confederates actually succeeded in driving some of the Federals back into the town, where they took refuge in the homes and buildings. As Mosgrove related, "They poured a galling fire into our ranks, and having no artillery we were unable to dislodge them. Had it been possible, we would have burned them out". The rain continued into the day. Martin had not been successful in turning the Federal flank, and after thirty minutes of fighting with the fortified Federals, the Confederate losses were mounting. The Confederates finally withdrew out the Lexington Pike, where four miles distant they found Martin's force, which had sustained severe losses. To the Confederate surprise, Burbridge did not pursue them down the Lexington Pike. As Mosgrove admitted, "The surprise was complete and our losses great. In the early morning the situation was depressing, tending to demoralization; but the phenomenally short time it took the troops to recover, get into line and coolly go into battle, challenged the respect and admiration of even the foe. Ordinary troops would probably have surrendered without firing a gun".

After the battle, the city hired Mr. Lee Orear's father to dig a grave and bury the Confederate dead. They were laid out in several layers. The mass grave is about on a northerly extension of the property line between 329 and 331 West Main Street, about 25 paces north of the north line of those properties. There is a large area slightly sunken. [37]

On July 11, 1864 General Jubal Early began an invasion of Washington, D.C. Union forces repelled Early's army on the outskirts of Washington on July 12. Lincoln becomes the first standing President to witness a battle.

On July 17, 1864 Confederate President Jefferson Davis replaced General Joseph E. Johnston with General

The War of Rebellion

John Bell Hood in hopes of defeating Union General William T. Sherman outside of Atlanta. After this the Military authorities thought it best to erect a small fort at Mount Sterling, and Captain Gunn and Captain Halstead were assigned the duty, and soon a very formidable little fort was built on the land of Mr. Dillard Hazelrigg, east of town, and across the Spencer Road from Machpelah cemetery. Fort Hill, as it was called, was located on the south side of Little Mountain Street – now called Locust Street – and occupied a corner of the Hazelrigg estate. [38] The report from the office of the US Engineers Agency, Armies of the West stated the following, "The fort was staked off at Mount Sterling upon the site opposite the cemetery on July 10, as directed by yourself, from the plan of the immediate locality I had surveyed and submitted to you. The amount of work done up to the 1st of September is 1,797 days' work of ten hours each. The work was done in three reliefs, but this is the net result reduced to regular days' work. As the result of this work the earth-work of the fort is thrown up to within a foot of its full height, and within two feet of its full thickness on an average. ....The platforms for the eight guns have been built and the magazine dug out". [39] After the completion of the fort there were no more demonstrations by the Rebels from the eastern part of the state.

     Again in September, 1864 General S.G. Burbridge organized another expedition down the Pound Gap Road to Saltville, Virginia where he was defeated on October 3rd. Another expedition was then undertaken in December under General Stoneman, and this time the Federals succeeded in capturing Saltville on December 20 – 21, 1864 and pushed the Rebels out of northwest Virginia. General Stoneman returned through Mount Sterling.

1865

The next few months were relatively quiet in Mount Sterling. Spring brought the news that on April 9th, 1865 Lee had surrendered and there was rejoicing among the Union people in the city. Hardly had the wave of good news flooded over the town, when another news flash swept the town that Abraham Lincoln has been assassinated.

Confederate soldiers began to surrender themselves to the appropriate Federal authorities, coming out of the mountains of eastern Kentucky into Mount Sterling. With the news of Robert E. Lee's surrender at Appomattox, the men of the Fourth Kentucky Confederate Cavalry were disheartened and undecided as to the next course of action. Some wanted to march to Mississippi and join Joseph E. Johnston's army. Others wanted to march to Mexico and never live under Federal control. Colonel Henry L. Giltner advised the men under his command in the Army of Southwest Virginia, with the Fourth Kentucky attached, that further resistance was fruitless, and that he intended to march to Kentucky from their camp in the mountains of Virginia and surrender as soon as possible. Many of the men then marched to Hazel Green and sent a flag of truce on to General Hobson in Mount Sterling to ascertain the terms of surrender that would be offered. The response was that basically the men would be offered the same terms as was granted to Lee. Immediately the Fourth Kentucky, with George Dallas Mosgrove included, marched to Mount Sterling and surrendered, where they were paroled on May 10, 1865. [40] In one report to Major-General Palmer from Brigadier General Hobson, dated April 28, 1865, stated, "The flag-of-truce party left Mount Sterling this morning. They accept our terms, with the exception of surrender of officer's horses. They have copy of terms and will submit them to Colonel Giltner, commanding, who is supposed to be beyond Mount Sterling. Scouts report no rebels within nine miles of the place. Am endeavoring to get mounted force to that place". [41]

With the end of hostilities, now began the long and slow process of rebuilding the charred remains of Mount Sterling and reviving its damaged economy.

Court Day

After Kentucky was admitted to the Union on June 1, 1792 as the fifteenth state, the General Assembly enacted a statute establishing the County Courts and provided that each court should meet monthly. Montgomery County was established on December 14, 1796 by an act of the General Assembly, and Mount Sterling soon became the official county seat. A year later the city had four retail stores and three taverns. By 1800 the city of Mount Sterling had a population of nearly 100 people, making it the eighteenth largest city in Kentucky.[1] In 1821 a statute was enacted directing the county courts to meet monthly on the same Monday of the month, and to continue the court until all the business of the term was completed. [2] Montgomery County adopted the custom of the County Court meeting on the third Monday of every month.

Membership in the county courts was vested with the magistrates, also known as the justices of the peace. The senior magistrate was elected as sheriff of the county. The magistrates performed a wide variety of functions including the trial of petty civil and criminal matters, the taking of depositions, the certifying of legal documents, and the impaneling of commissions to inspect the turnpikes. The magistrates received no salaries as members of the county court, but they were entitled to fees for their services as magistrates. Initially the magistrates were appointed as members of the county court for life. [3]

The early magistrates in each county were the community leaders, in most cases they were landowners with substantial holdings, and some were Revolutionary War veterans, pioneers or officers in the state militia. They represented the wealthier stratus of the community. By the middle of the 1800s, on average eighty percent of the magistrates were farmers, six percent were lawyers, and the balance were merchants, manufacturers, tavern keepers and tradesmen. Their power and influence naturally extended into the political arena, and during this same period of time on average nearly twenty-five percent of the state I Legislature was composed of magistrates from the various counties. [4]

The influence of the county courts cut a broad swath and impacted the lives of every citizen in the county. The non-judicial business of the county court was wide-ranging including such subjects as county roads, milldams, ferries, taxes and levies, the establishment of towns, patronage, emancipation, guardianship of orphans, the poor and the vagrant, and the licensing of taverns. The majority of the court's time was spent on the judicial matters related to probating wills and the administration of estates, including the settling of the accounts of the executor and the division of property. [5] Due to all of these activities of the court, everyone was interested in the monthly business of the court, and they were drawn to the county seat on the appointed Monday to learn first-hand about the current business. The court's greatest virtue, it's inexpensiveness with no pay to the magistrates, led to its downfall.

The county court system was eventually reformed for several reasons. Most magistrates were not lawyers and did not educate themselves in the subtleties of their judicial business. With no salaries, persistent inattention to the duties of the court plagued the system. County voters and taxpayers had no express role in the selection of court members or in the formation of county policy. In most cases courts filled their own vacancies without consulting their constituency. Although the business of the Governor and the legislature was filled with complaints from the various counties over the operation of the courts, the legislature failed to deal meaningfully with the original shortcomings of the county court system. And the impact of the two-party political system, which organized the factional bickering that plagued the county courts, stressed more than ever politicking over performance. [6]

Montgomery County has a tradition of holding in high esteem its county court judges and members of the bar.

Some of the most prominent families in the county have been involved with the legal profession. Names such as Apperson, Chiles, Grubbs, Holt, Lane, O'Rear, Prewitt, Reid and Winn are highly regarded, and these men and others are noted jurists and community leaders. Many of the streets of Mount Sterling, and even individual residences, bear their names in recognition of the leadership and power that they held, and the honor bestowed upon them by the community.

The original boundaries of Montgomery County were significantly broader than those that delineate the county today. In the early days there were large distances to be traveled over poor dirt roads to come to Mount Sterling to attend to the court's business. This eventually led to the creation of new counties with shorter travel distances to the county seat. The "rule of thumb" to determine a reasonable travel distance was that a man should be able to ride from his home to the county seat and back in a single day.

The reader can imagine that in those early days the business of the court could be addressed in relatively short order, leaving a good deal of idle time for those who had "come to town". And since in some cases the distances seemed rather great given the time it took to travel over the dirt roads in poor condition that lead to Mount Sterling from the extensive reaches of the county, the visitors to Mount Sterling undoubtedly stayed over for a few days. They discussed items of concern such as local and national politics, the workings of their own county court, and they purchased their supplies to take home.

James Lane Allen wrote in Harpers New Monthly Magazine in 1889, "But after all the business was over, time still hung idly on their hands, and being vigorous men, hardened by work in forest and field, trained in foot and limb to fleetness and endurance, and fired with admiration of physical prowess, like riotous school-boys out on a half-holiday, they fell to playing. All through the first quarter of the century, and for a longer time, county court day in Kentucky was, at least in many parts of the State, the occasion for holding athletic games. The men, young or in the sinewy manhood of more than middle age, assembled once a month at the county-seats to witness and take part in the feats of muscle and courage". Mr. Allen goes on to explain, "But after all, this was only play, and play never is perfectly satisfying to a man who would rather fight; so from playing they fell to the harder work, with a more indemnifying motive, and throughout the period county court day was the monthly Monday on which the Kentuckian regularly did his fighting. It was periodical, and could be relied upon, being written in the law, noted in the almanac, and registered in the heavens". [7] So court day became the regularly scheduled date for settling real or perceived injustices on a man-to-man basis, and fighting openly in the streets became a normal feature. "Thus the justices sat quietly on the bench inside, and the people fought quietly in the streets outside, and the day of all the month set apart for the conservation of the peace became the approved day for carrying on individual war. There is no evidence to be had that either the justices or the constables ever interfered". But when it was over for the day, it was over for the month. "The fight over, all animosity was gone, the feud ended. The men must shake hands, go and drink together, become friends".

As the official business of Montgomery County grew in importance, and as more and more people were drawn to Mount Sterling on the third Monday of the month, several changes gradually occurred. The third Monday of the month drew more business to the local merchants than any other day of the month. The crowds in the little town continued to grow. The growing crowds were noted by the politicians, who took advantage of the opportunity to campaign and give speeches. "Doctors" began selling elixirs of every type on the street corners, and the visitors took the opportunity to do a little trading amongst themselves.

Everyone was drawn to the Court House. Horses were hitched to thick iron rings embedded in the stone wall around the Court House yard. Troughs were at the ends for watering the horses. It cost ten cents to hitch up all day. [8] The farmers brought their produce into town to sell at the "market" on Court Day. Livestock was beginning to be traded in rather large volumes. Mules, horses, oxen, dogs, hogs, sheep, turkeys and geese were herded into the middle of town in a cacophony of noise amid the animated trading between those who had come to town to conduct legal, political and economic business. Street sanitation was all but forgotten for one day each month.

In the old days the scene was described as follows: "The town is packed. It looks as though by some vast suction system it had with one exercise of force drawn all the county life into itself. The poor dumb creatures gathered in from the peaceful fields, and crowded around the Court House, send forth, each after its own kind, a general outcry of horror and despair at the tumult of the scene and the unimaginable mystery of their own fate. They quite overflow into the by-streets, where they take possession of the sidewalks, and debar entrance at private residences. As the day draws near noon, the tide of life is at full flood. All mixed in with the tossing of horns and nimble heels of the terrified, distressed, half-maddened beasts, are the people. At the corners of the streets long-haired – and long-eared – doctors in curious hats lecture to eager groups on maladies and philanthropic cures. Every itinerant vender of notion and nostrum in the country-side is there. Strangely contrasted with everything else in physical type and marks of civilization are the mountaineers, who have come down to "the settlements" driving herds of their lean, stunted cattle, or bringing, in slow-moving, oxen-drawn "steamboat" wagons, maple-sugar, and baskets, and poles, and wild mountain fruit – faded wagons, faded beasts, faded clothes, faded faces, faded everything. A general day of buying and selling". [9]

The October Court Day in Mount Sterling has always drawn the largest crowds. Before winter set in, and while the roads were still passable, people would come down from the mountains over the Pound Gap Road, and from the surrounding counties in every direction to sell the produce from the summer harvest and to buy and trade for the supplies that they would need for the winter. They would buy, sell

Typical Court Day in Mount Sterling, Kentucky. Pictured is Maysville Street looking north alongside the Court House.

Post Civil War Court House in Mount Sterling. This Court House stood until 1890 when it was replaced with another building on the same site.

"Concluding a Bargain" from Harper's New Monthly Magazine, August, 1889.

"Swapping Horses" from Harper's New Monthly Magazine, August, 1889

Court Day

and trade for such items as guns, knives, tools, ax handles, sorghum molasses, wicker chairs, mules, horses, dogs, food, clothing, household items, whiskey and coal. The second largest crowd always gathered for the third Monday in February when supplies had run low from the winter and new supplies were needed for the spring. [a] The February Court Day became an especially big trading day for mules and work horses as farmers were preparing for the spring and summer work. Southern buyers were on hand to buy mules to ship by flatboat down the Mississippi River to work in the cotton and cane fields.

The April Court Day was like a horse show. The fancy horse trade was particularly brisk. Montgomery County was famous for the fine saddle horses and trotters. A handsome horse was the greatest pride of a Kentuckian, and the owner delighted in riding around town 'just showing off his fine horse'. Any farmer owned 10 to 50 horses. [10]

After the 1870s when the railroad arrived to Mount Sterling, the trade increased with merchants purchasing goods and shipping them to other cities. Noted, for example, were "3000 geese to be shipped to New York fed on the William Sutton farm and caused much confusion as they were driven through the streets of Mount Sterling". Another example included, "450 hogs were shipped to Baltimore from Court Day". There was also a large increase in the volume of goods coming to market in Mount Sterling from distant locations. One newspaper article stated, "2000 hogs were driven in from Missouri for Court Day". Other products exported from Mount Sterling included sheep, hemp, tobacco, whiskey, skins and Indian Corn". [11 b]

Various reminisces handed down regarding the early Court Days include: Dust everywhere, or mud, knee deep, depending on the weather; 18-inch plank sidewalks around the Court House; spurts of tobacco juice; women holding up their ankle length skirts as they crossed the streets, the men enjoying the scene, and being free with their comments; snuff users; some people bringing lunch and staying all day, some sitting on the street eating cheese and crackers and dill pickles bought in the grocery; chairs in the back of jolt wagons for the women to ride; dog stealing; drunks; crowded taverns, each with an expert mixologist; pure copper whiskey at twenty-five cents a gallon; trading, and fantastic stories of good and bad deals; and "the prettiest girls in the world were right here in Mount Sterling". [12]

And now in the twenty-first century, some things about Court Day have changed, and yet it remains the same. The very name of the day no longer brings to mind the image of the Court House and the judge on the bench. There are no celebrations in February or April, or any other month except for October. The day is no longer the gathering day for the business of the county. The men do not come to Court Day to pick a fight or settle an argument. Men no longer walk around the town armed – except those who are trading old flintlock Kentucky long rifles, shotguns, pistols and pocket knives. The day is no longer a general market day for the county residents and their neighbors in the surrounding counties. Drinking in the taverns (although admittedly still popular with a portion of the residents) is no longer the primary pass-time of the visitors to Mount Sterling on Court Day. Patent medicine and peddlers no longer roam the streets, but rather they are organized into booth spaces along Locust Street.

But through all these changes, one thing remains the same: the people in Montgomery County will come to Court Day. Maybe it is for the same reason that people are drawn to train wrecks and fires, or maybe it is because they instinctively are attracted to the swarm of people and the large gatherings – especially the outdoor sort of gathering. It is like the county fair, only better because when the Montgomery County native leaves the swarm of Court Day he feels satisfied. Yes, he is drawn to it. He is drawn to the sights and smells and sounds of the crowd. He will walk among the booths and look for that special bargain that he may want. He will make his small purchases, view all the goods, and mingle in the crush of people in the narrow streets of the town just as his fathers did before him.

Court Day

A good summary of the current October Court Day festival was published in the October 22, 1969 edition of the Mount Sterling Advocate – the local newspaper. "The crowd is a melting pot of politicians and preachers, sun bonnets and short skirts, of overhauls and business suits, of crew cuts and hippie hair styles, of gaudy slacks and tight fitting denims, of sandals, work shoes and bare feet. There were old, and they also travel in baby buggies. They came in all shapes, sizes and fashions".

Today's October Court Day festival, held during the weekend of the third Monday in October, became a three day event in 1971. Estimates indicate that nearly 100,000 people will visit Mount Sterling during these three days. They will come from all over Kentucky, and as many as twenty different States, to buy and sell antiques and home-grown mountain goods. They jam the streets and become part of the swarm and tax the city's ability to cope. They search for parking, they search for food, they search for facilities, and they search among the junk to find the treasures. And that is part of the charm of October Court Day in Mount Sterling, Kentucky.

Notes

The Mounds of Montgomery County
And the Earliest Inhabitants of the Area

[1] "Traces of the Earliest Inhabitants" 15 Dec. 2004 <http://www.kentuckygenealogy.org/todd/traces_of_the_earliest_inhabitants.htm>

[2] Robert Silverberg, The Mound Builders, (New York: Ballentine, 1970) 28 – 29

[3] Bennett Young, "Prehistoric Men in Kentucky," The Filson Club, (Louisville), 1910. Pages 3 – 5

[4] Allen W. Eckert, The Frontiersmen, (Boston: Little, Brown & Co, 1967) 65 – 66

[5] W.D. Funkhouser and W.S. Webb, Reports in Archaeology and Anthropology, Volume II, (Lexington: University of Kentucky Press, 1935) 297 – 302

[6] Lewis Collins, History of Kentucky, (Covington, Kentucky: Re-Print by Clearfield Company, Baltimore 1995, Volume 2, 1874) 633

[7] Silverberg 124

[8] LucienBeckner, "The Moundbuilders", The Filson Club History Quarterly, (Louisville: Vol 29, July 1955) 206 – 207

[9] William S. Webb and Charles E. Snow, The Adena People (Knoxville: The University of Tennessee Press, 1974) 12 – 15

[10] Webb and Snow 264

[11] Webb and Snow 35

[12] Silverberg 120-121

[13] Silverberg 146

[14] "Holocaust of Giants, The Great Smithsonian Cover-up" 15 Dec. 2004,<http://www.xpeditionsmagazine.com/magazine/articles/giants/holocaust.html>

[15] Silverberg 28

[16] "Holocaust of Giants, The Great Smithsonian Cover-up"

[17] Silverberg 102 –103

[18] Silverberg 109

[19] Lyman C. Draper Manuscripts, 29CC30-31

[20] W.D. Funkhouser and W.S. Webb, Reports in Archaeology and Anthropology, Volume III, Number 3: The Ricketts Site (Lexington: University of Kentucky Press, July, 1935) 71 - 73

[21] Funkhouser and Webb, 73 – 79

[22] Webb and Snow, 13 – 28

[23] W.D. Funkhouser and W.S. Webb, Reports in Archaeology and Anthropology, Volume II, 303 - 309

Notes

[24] Judge Caswell Lane (personal communication, February 2, 2005)

[25] Webb and Snow, 31 – 33

Indian Old Fields

[1] Patsy Woodring, "Indian Old Fields, Home of the Shawnee" 31 Dec. 2004, http://kentuckyexplorer.com/nonmembers/01-04020.html

[2] Lucien Beckner, "John Findley: The First Pathfinder of Kentucky", The Filson Club History Quarterly, (Louisville: Vol 1, No. 3 April, 1927) 111 – 121

[3] Patsy Woodring, "Indian Old Fields, Home of the Shawnee"

[4] A. Gwynn Henderson, Cynthia E. Jobe, Christopher A. Turnbow, "Indian Occupation and Use in Northern and Eastern Kentucky During the Contact Period (1540 – 1795): An Initial Investigation", submitted to The Kentucky Heritage Council, (March, 1986) 82 – 85

[5] Lyman C. Draper Manuscripts, 11CC88.

[6] Draper, 11CC95-97

[7] Draper, 11CC97

[8] Draper, 11CC93

[9] Lucien Beckner, "The Moundbuilders", The Filson Club History Quarterly, (Lousiville: Vol 29, No 3 July, 1955) 208

[10] Lucien Beckner, "The Moundbuilders", 208

[11] Patsy Woodring, "Indian Old Fields, Home of the Shawnee"

[12] LucienBeckner, "Eskippakithiki: The Last Indian Town in Kentucky", The Filson Club History Quarterly, (Louisville: Vol 6, October, 1932) 367 – 368

Notes

Estill's Defeat

[1] Bessie Taul Conkright, "Estill's Defeat or The Battle of Little Mountain", Register Kentucky State Historical Society, (Louisville: Vol 22, 1924) 311
[2] William Chenault, (1882, August 27). Madison County. Interesting Sketch of Pioneer Days. The Courier-Journal: Louisville. Letter to the editor. Page 12.
[3] Elizabeth Perkins, Border Life – Experience and Memory in the Revolutionary Ohio Valley, (Chapel Hill: The University of North Carolina Press, 1998), 67-68, 78
[4] William Chenault
[5] Lyman C. Draper Manuscripts, 13C51
[6] Lyman C. Draper Manuscripts, 13C51
[7] Bessie Taul Conkright, 310
[8] Bessie Taul Conkright, 312
[9] Bessie Taul Conkright, 312 – 313
[10] William Chenault
[11] Bessie Taul Conkright, 313 – 314
[12] Lyman C. Draper Manuscripts, 13C51
[13] Bessie Taul Conkright, 313 – 314
[14] Dillard Hazelrigg, letter to Lymon C. Draper, April 29, 1842, Draper Manuscripts 13C50
[15] Deposition of Joseph Rogers, March, 1804, Thomas Mosely vs. John Harmon et al, lawsuit regarding disputed land claims. The deposition on page 198 reads, "Deposition of Joseph Rogers (taken on March 30, 1804, at the place where James Estill was killed in Montgomery County, before James Turley and John Roberts): That he was engaged in the battle with Captain James Estill against the Indians the time said Estill was killed and that he is now at or near the spot where James Estill was killed which is laid down on the platt by Mr. Fall, surveyor, as will appear by reference to the platt designated by the letter "e" and further saith that he saw an Indian catch and kill James Estill at this spot of ground and on the third day after the battle was fought he returned to this place with a company of men which he supposed to be about 40 or 50 men to bury the dead and found James Estill dead on this spot of ground".
[16] Bessie Taul Conkright, 320
[17] David Cook, Account of Estill's Defeat appearing in Hunt's Western Review, (June, 1820, William Hunt, editor)
[18] WH Perrin, JH Butler, GC Knifen, History of Kentucky Illustrated, (Louisville: FA Battery Publishing Company, 1887) 180
[19] James Berry, deposition, Conley's Heirs vs Chiles, Kentucky Court of Appeals, Madison County, Kentucky, 1831

[20] Lymon C. Draper Manuscripts, 13C51
[21] Bessie Taul Conkright, 316
[22] Lyman C. Draper Manuscripts, 13C58; (1874, February 14) "The Battle of Little Mountain – Estill's Defeat", *The Courier-Journal*: Louisville
[23] Bessie Taul Conkright, 318
[24] Lymon C. Draper Manuscripts, 12CC222-225; Survey by Robert Morrow dated September 16, 1817 in the case of Thomas Morrow vs. John Harmon et al filed in the Fayette Circuit Court.
[25] William Chenault
[26] Lewis Collins, 635
[27] WH Perrin, JH Butler, GC Knifen, 180 – 181
[28] Bessie Taul Conkright, 317
[29] Bessie Taul Conkright, 318 – 319
[30] WH Perrin, JH Butler, GC Knifen, 180 – 181
[31] Bessie Taul Conkright, 318 – 319
[32] WH Perrin, JH Butler, GC Knifen, 180 – 181
[33] Bessie Taul Conkright, 319
[34] David Cook, Account of Estill's Defeat appearing in Hunt's Western Review, (June, 1820, William Hunt, editor)
[35] Bessie Taul Conkright, 319 - 320
[36] Bessie Taul Conkright, 321
[37] Bessie Taul Conkright, 319
[38] William Chenault
[39] Lewis Collins, 636

Notes

Morgan's Station

[1] Harry G. Enoch, In Search of Morgan's Station and "The Last Indian Raid in Kentucky" (Bowie, Maryland: Heritage Books, Inc, 1997) 20

[2] Harry G. Enoch, 27 – 29
[3] Harry G. Enoch, 30
[4] Harry G. Enoch, 30 – 34
[5] Lyman C. Draper Manuscripts, 12CC 11-41, Interview No. 1 with James Wade In Bath County, Kentucky.
[6] Lyman C. Draper Manuscripts, 12CC 11-41
[7] Harry G. Enoch, 52 – 61
[8] Harry G. Enoch, 63 – 64
[9] Harry G. Enoch, 64 – 65
[10] Harry G. Enoch, 69
[11] Harry G. Enoch, 70 – 71
[12] Lyman C. Draper Manuscripts, 12CC 55 - 57, Interview with Col. James Lane
[13] "Historic Shawnee Names of the 1700's", Don Greene, March 27, 2005 www.shawnee-traditions.com
[14] Allen W. Eckert, The Frontiersmen, 392 – 393
[15] Harry G. Enoch, 85 – 86
[16] Harry G. Enoch, 87 – 88
[17] Harry G. Enoch, 89
[18] Harry G. Enoch, 94
[19] Harry G. Enoch, 99 – 100
[20] Allen W. Eckert, The Frontiersmen, 393 – 394
[21] Allen W. Eckert, The Frontiersmen, 393 – 394
[22] Allen W. Eckert, The Frontiersmen, 393 – 395
[23] Harry G. Enoch, 106 – 107
[24] Harry G. Enoch, 104
[25] Harry G. Enoch, 114
[26] Harry G. Enoch, 109, 133 - 134
[27] Morgan / McCullough genealogy, March 15, 2005. http://www.geocities.com/heartland/5248/sutton2/WC06/WC06_225.htm

Montgomery County and The War of Rebellion

[1] John Marshall Prewitt, "Montgomery County During the Civil War, Notes on Locations, and Sources of Information", undated manuscript.
[2] Charles S. Adams, "Cincinnati's Forgotten General", http://users.aol.com/dmsmith001/adams.htm, May 8, 2005
[3] Dr. John Magarvey Prewitt, "The Civil War in Montgomery County", undated manuscript, 1937.
[4] John Marshall Prewitt
[5] Geoge Dallas Mosgrove, Kentucky Cavaliers in Dixie, Lincoln: The University of Nebraska Press, 1999, 40.
[6] John Marshall Prewitt
[7] Thomas W. Parsons, Incidents & Experiences in the Life of Thomas W. Parsons, Lexington: The University of Kentucky Press, 1975. 95 – 97
[8] John Marshall Prewitt
[9] Thomas W. Parsons, 95 – 96
[10] George Dallas Mosgrove, Kentucky Cavaliers in Dixie, Lincoln: University of Nebraska Press, 1999. 122 - 123
[11] Thomas W. Parsons, page 100
[12] Carl B. Boyd, Jr. and Hazel Mason Boyd, A History of Mt. Sterling, Kentucky, 1792 – 1918, 1984. 45
[13] www.ehistory.com/uscw/library/or/023/0871.cfm, Official Records, The War of Rebellion: Chapter XXVIII, 871 May 9, 2005
[14] George Dallas Mosgrove, 41
[15] www.ehistory.com/uscw/library/or/023/0876.cfm, Official Records, The War of Rebellion: Chapter XXVIII, 876 May 9, 2005
[16] Thomas W. Parsons, 106 – 108
[17] Thomas W. Parsons, 110 – 111
[18] Thomas W. Parsons, 111
[19] Bennett H. Young, Confederate Wizards of the Saddle, Boston: Chapple Publishing Company, 1914. 171-173
[20] Bennett H. Young, 175
[21] Thomas W. Parsons, 117 – 118
[22] Bennett H. Young, 178 – 180
[23] Thomas W. Parsons, 118 – 119
[24] Bennett H. Young, 181.
[25] www.ehistory.com/uscw/library/or/034/0162.cfm, May 9, 2005, Official Records, The War of Rebellion: Chapter XXXV, 162 – 163: Report from General Q.A. Gillmore to Major-General Horatio G. Wright dated March 23, 1863.
[26] Bennett H. Young, 183 – 185
[27] Thomas W. Parsons, 121
[28] John Marshall Prewitt
[29] Dr. John McGarvey Prewitt

[30] Bennett H. Young, 188 – 189
[31] www.ehistory.com/usew/library/or/034/0162.cfm May 9, 2005, Official Records, The War of Rebellion: Chapter XXIII, 163 – 164
[32] Thomas W. Parsons, 139
[33] Thomas W. Parsons, 140
[34] Thomas W. Parsons, 140
[35] Thomas W. Parsons, 141
[36] John Marshall Prewitt
[37] John Marshall Prewitt
[38] Thomas W. Parsons, 142
[39] www.ehistory.com/usew/library/or/078/0387.cfm, May 9, 2005, Official Records, The War of Rebellion: Chapter XXXIX, 387.
[40] George Dallas Mosgrove, 264
[41] www.ehistory.com/usew/library/or/104/0510.cfm May 9, 2005, Official Records, The War of Rebellion: Chapter XLIZ, page 510.

Court Day

[1] Carl B. Boyd, Jr. and Hazel Mason Boyd, A History of Mt. Sterling, Kentucky, 1792 – 1918, 1984. 5-6
[2] Robert M. Ireland, The County Courts in Antebellum Kentucky, (Lexington, The University of Kentucky Press, 1972) 10
[3] Robert M. Ireland, 7 – 11
[4] Robert M. Ireland, 14
[5] Robert M. Ireland, 18 – 19
[6] Robert M. Ireland, 172 – 174
[7] James Lane Allen, "County Court Day in Kentucky", Harper's New Monthly Magazine (New York: Harper and Brothers, Vol 79, August, 1889) 386 – 388
[8] Sarah Alice Harris, Montgomery County, Kentucky bicentennial, 1774 – 1974, (Mount Sterling, 1975). 111
[9] James Lane Allen, 390
[10] Sarah Alice Harris, 111
[11] Sarah Alice Harris, 111
[12] Sarah Alice Harris, 112

Author's Notes

The Mounds of Montgomery County

[a] There is also an Indian tradition that Ohio and Kentucky had once been inhabited by a race of white people. Allen Eckert in <u>The Frontiersmen</u> relates that Chief Cornstalk, the principal chief of the Chalahgawtha Shawnee, is said to have stated to Colonel William McKee when he commanded forces on the Kanawha River in West Virginia, that the Ohio and Kentucky territories had once been inhabited by a white people "who were familiar with the arts" of which the Indians knew nothing. He said that after a series of battles the whites had been completely eliminated. Cornstalk said that the old forts had not been built by the Indians but had been built by a "very long ago" people who were white in complexion, and "skilled in the arts". He also said that the old burial places were the graves of an unknown people.

Eckert quotes a second source of this tale in his book <u>That Dark and Bloody River</u>. Shawnee Chief Black Fish is said to have related a similar story to Captain Thomas Bullitt. Black Fish said that "the Kan-tuck-kee land is not owned by the Shawnee. It belongs to the ghosts of the murdered Azgens – a white people from an eastern sea". He said that their bones and ghosts occupy every hill and valley of the country, and that they protect the game there because they do not need or use material food for themselves. He said, "long ago our fathers killed off the Azgens".

[b] Constantine Samuel Rafinesque was born in 1783 in the city of Constantinople, and by 1804 he was a noted naturalist in the United States who had come to the attention of President Thomas Jefferson. He was a professor at Transylvania University in Lexington, Kentucky from 1819 to 1826, and identified 148 prehistoric Indian sites in Kentucky during this time. Another site, visited by Professor Rafinesque in 1819 situated near Mt. Sterling is described by Collins as, "The site consisted of a large truncated mound, 25 feet in height, flanked on the north and west by narrow grades or slopes. It was connected with a circular work, 350 feet in diameter, by an elevated way or terrace, 100 feet long. The circle had a small mound in its center, and a gateway opening to the east. Three small mounds occur in connection". When the author visited the Camargo site in March, 2006 he was able to locate the site and probably one of the circles or earthworks. Also, by 2005 the University of Kentucky had for the most part closed their exhibits of the artifacts taken from the scores of Indian mounds in Kentucky. The author was granted permission to see the Gaitskill tablets and the Wright tablet stored at the University of Kentucky Department of Anthropology in Lexington, Kentucky.

The Early History of Montgomery County, Kentucky

Indian Old Fields

[a] It is now generally thought that there were no Indians permanently residing in Kentucky at the time that Boone and Finley first viewed the Bluegrass. However, references from some early settlers at least make mention of semi-permanent Indian towns. An early fur trader named Alexander Maginty was noted to be returning from a trading tour to the Cuttawas Indians in the Carolinas and was "encamped on the southern bank of the Cantucky River, about twenty-five miles from the Blue Lick Town," which may have also been called Little Pict Town, the Pioneer's name for a village of the Piqua division of the Shawnee. Whatever the name, the approximate location of the town referenced by Maginty would be in the area of Indian Old Fields. Maginty was traveling on the Warrior's Trace.

In 1832, Simon Kenton said in an interview with John James that "The Indians never made but two settlements in Kentucky, one on Slate Creek, and one at the place called Lul-be-grud; and at both places they raised corn". (Lyman C Draper Manuscripts, 5BB122).

In current Richmond, Kentucky it has been noted that the remains of an old Indian town stood near the place where the present Courthouse is located, and that Town Fork of the Dreaming Creek takes its name from the remains of the old Indian town. There are also several notable Indian mounds located in the city of Richmond. This site was probably well known to the early settlers along Muddy Creek in 1775, given that it was less than four miles away.

[b] According to Patsy Woodring, after founding Boonesborough in the spring of 1775, Daniel Boone invited Thomas Goff to hunt with him in the Eskippakithiki area, where they narrowly avoided detection from several Indians who were hunting deer. By 1800 Goff had settled in the immediate area of the old Indian village. In the War of 1812 Elisha Goff and Leonard Beall joined the ranks of the Clark County contingent. Beall was captured by the Indian allies of the British at the Battle of Raisin River near Detroit, and sentenced to run the gauntlet. The old Shawnee chief, Black Hoof, whose Shawnee name was Catahekassa, let him go when he heard that Beall was born in Eskippakithiki. He took Beall to his cabin and claimed him as a son. Black Hoof wanted to hear all about the place where he was born and lived until middle age. Beall invited Black Hoof to visit his Kentucky home, and Beall was subsequently released and returned home. In the summer of 1816 the aged Black Hoof came walking in barefooted from an Indian reservation in Ohio. He pointed out to the white settlers many places of interest in the former village. He told the settlers that while he was fighting in the French and Indian War he had shot repeatedly at George Washington, but was never able to hit him. He decided that Washington bore a charmed life. Black Hoof died in Ohio in 1831.

Author's Notes

^c According to Ted Franklin Belue in <u>The Hunters of Kentucky</u>, this was actually Steven Ruddell, who at this time had become a minister and was known as Pastor Ruddell. As a young man Ruddell had been captured by the Indians in June, 1780 when Colonel Byrd led 600 Wyandotte and Shawnee Indians and about 30 British soldiers in the attack on Ruddle's Station and Martin's Station near the Licking River. When he finally was returned to his parents nearly a decade later, Steven spoke broken English, wore leggings and a clout and ear-bobs, and had an Indian wife and several children. He was fluent in the Algonquin language spoken by the Shawnee. After he had reconverted to white ways he became a minister, but retained the fluency of his second tongue.

^d According to James Adair's <u>History of the American Indians</u>, published in London, England in 1775, each Indian nation had either a house or town of refuge that was distant from the primary villages; that the house or village was a sure asylum to protect a man-slayer, and that these sites were not necessarily permanently occupied. The returning warrior who had killed an enemy was seldom allowed to return directly home until an elder or chief decided that sufficient time had passed (for fear of the sure retribution of blood-for-blood that was common among the Indians), or that the proper observance of the purification ritual over several days had been conducted. The ritual in some cases consisted of a three-day stay in a "hot house" (a type of sauna) where the warrior would purify himself with warm lotions and fasted the entire time, having only ritualistic boiled root beverages during this time. Adair added further that, "In almost every Indian nation, there are several peaceable towns, which are called "old-beloved," "ancient, holy, or white towns;" they seem to have been formerly "towns of refuge," for it is not in the memory of their oldest people, that ever human blood was shed in them; although they often force persons from thence, and put them to death elsewhere."

The author points out that Indian Old Fields was situated along the heavily-traveled Warrior's Path near a major intersection of the Path; that in historic times in Kentucky there were no permanent Indian villages, and the author speculates that it may be possible that the site was used at various times as a town of refuge by one or more Indian nations.

James Adair was a trader from South Carolina who lived among the Cherokee and Chickasaws in Tennessee, the Creeks in Georgia, and the Choctaws in Mississippi from 1736 to about 1768. His first-hand accounts and observations of the Indians were published in <u>History of the American Indians</u> in London, England in 1775. The first English settlements in Kentucky and Tennessee were not established until the 1770s. At the time that Adair was living and trading among the Indians, he observed that many of the customs, traditions and religious practices of the Indians were in decline and in a state of corruption, and that the customs and traditions were observed mostly by the older people.

Estill's Defeat

[a] A brief chronology of events in Kentucky prior to Estill's battle with a band of Wyandotte Indians on March 22, 1782 helps place context around the significance that this battle had on the Kentucky frontier in 1782:

i. June, 1774 Harrodsburg started, and abandoned in the Fall. Escalation of hostilities with the Indians – started by Jacob Greathouse and the massacre of the family of Chief Logan near Fort Pitt – results in Lord Dunmore's War. D. Boone and M. Stoner sent to warn the surveyor's of the impending danger.
ii. October 10, 1774 Battle of Point Pleasant. Virginia's British Governor, Lord Dunmore, devises a plan to keep Virginia out of the coming revolution by instigating the Ohio Valley Indians to attack the Virginia frontier, thus keeping Virginians too busy defending themselves from the Indians to fight in the revolution.
iii. March, 1775 Boonesborough is established, despite attacks from Shawnees
iv. March, 1775 Hinkson Station (near Harrison County / Bourbon County line) started; abandoned in summer of 1776.
v. April, 1775 McClelland's Station (Georgetown, Kentucky) established
vi. April 20, 1775 Battles of Concord and Lexington, Massachusetts, initiating American Revolution
vii. Fall, 1775 William Calk, Enoch Smith, Abraham Hanks, Robert Whitledge and Philip Drake explore Montgomery County following buffalo trail from Boonesborough. They find a huge Indian Mound, name it Little Mountain. Area is surveyed and land claims are made.
viii. 1776 Hugh Forbes claims land on Grassy Lick Creek. Purchased 1000 acres of land along Hinkston Creek. Land later to become the city named by Hugh Forbes, Mount Sterling.
ix. May 23, 1776 Indians attack Boonesborough
x. March 7, 1777 Shawnees under Chief Black Fish lay siege to Harrodsburg.

Author's Notes

[b] According to Lymon Draper in The Life of Daniel Boone, William Miller was reportedly born in Virginia on March 30, 1747 and settled on Paint Lick Creek (south of Estill's Station) in 1776. He was 35 years old at the battle of Estill's Defeat. He served on Clarke's campaign against the Indians in Ohio in 1782, was subsequently a colonel of the militia, and died at his residence on the west side of Paint Lick Creek, Garrard County, Kentucky on August 30, 1841 in the ninety-third year of his life. He was six feet, two inches in height, fair complexion, sparse frame, and pleasing countenance, possessing a kind and benevolent disposition.

[c] According to John Marshall Prewitt, local historian, he related in a telephone interview on January 29, 2005 a legend that the Indian Chief was not from the Wyandotte tribe, but rather from some neighboring tribe. After failing to raise the men from his own village to go on the raid to Kentucky, the Chief gathered the warriors from a neighboring Wyandotte village. In his book The Hunters of Kentucky, Ted Franklin Belue identifies the Indian Chief as Sourehoowah, and that his second in command was a young man named Split Log who wore red leggings. However, a quick check at the internet site www.shawnee-traditions.com reveals that Split Log's Shawnee name was Sounehueway, which so closely resembles the name used by Belue for the Chief as to cast doubt on the certainty of the name. Split Log, also known as Thomas Split Log, succeeded Round Head as principal chief of the Wyandottes in 1816. His brother in law was Tecumseh. Split Log was about 17 years old at the battle with Estill.

[d] John Marshall Prewitt further related that the spot where Estill fell was afterwards a well known surveyor's point, and marked the property line between two farms. There was a rock and concrete monument on the site marking where Estill was buried. Today the west-bound lane of I-64 runs directly over the spot where Estill fell. There reportedly is a bronze plaque along the fencerow of the west bound lane, near a big green interstate sign at the end of a row of guardrail and down a steep embankment. The Interstate runs directly over the branch where the battle was fought. During construction of the road, the flow of the various creeks that marked the battleground had been redirected, or in some cases covered over completely. Hinkston Creek, which had a natural bend at the sight of the battleground, has had the route straightened during the road construction. A map of the Kentucky Highway Department notes a concrete and stone monument with a bronze plaque at the site. When Mr. Prewitt pointedly informed the Kentucky Highway Commissioner in Frankfort that they were constructing I-64 directly over the Estill's Defeat battleground, the Commissioner – who understood the historical importance of the battle ground – told Mr. Prewitt, "If we were building this highway in Virginia, we would end up knocking down the Washington Monument"!

[e] In a telephone interview with Reverend Robert W. Estill of Raleigh, North Carolina, he indicated that he was at one point – until he had a son – the last living direct male descendent of James Estill. He told the story how as a small boy he and his parents had traveled to Richmond, Kentucky where he "pulled the sheet off" (or unveiled) the statue of James Estill in the Richmond Cemetery. He stated that upon Monk's return to Estill's Station, he was given his freedom, making him the first slave freed in Kentucky. Reverend Estill indicated that Monk was a short man – maybe 5 feet 3 inches – and weighed about 250 pounds. Monk remained in the Richmond, Kentucky area and had nine or ten children, most of whom were educated through the equivalent of High School, which was terrifically beyond any expectations for that time.

Reverend Estill also indicated that Kate Breckinridge – wife of John Marshall Prewitt – is a cousin of his, and the Breckinridge's and the Estill's were closely related in Kentucky history. Reverend Estill knows John Marshall Prewitt, and performed their wedding ceremony. Kate Breckinridge Prewitt (noted in the preceding sentence) is the great granddaughter of John C. Breckinridge, who was Vice-President of the United States from 1857 to 1861 under President James Buchanan, and a senator in the US Senate. Her grandmother's maiden name was Martha Rodes Estill, and she married David Prewitt. Robert Rhodes Estill was Kathy Dalton's grand-father (Mrs Lyle Dalton of Lexington, Kentucky). He had a brother named Robert Julian Estill.

At one time the Estill family owned a great deal of property on the Winchester Road that extended from east of Lexington near what is now I-75 all the way into Clark County near the city of Winchester.

Author's Notes

Morgan's Station

[a] In a telephone interview on February 2, 2005 with Judge Cas Lane, he indicated that his family are descendents of Colonel James Lane. Colonel Lane was a nephew of Enoch Smith, and he lived out near the Springfield Church. In addition, Georgia Prewitt's mother's maiden name was Lane, and according to Mrs. Prewitt, Colonel Lane was the great-great-great-grandfather of both Georgia Prewitt and Judge Cas Lane.

[b] On March 19, 2005 the author visited the Morgan's Station site. The spring that is contained in the springhouse is still running with sweet, cold water. The land must look much as it did at the time of the settlement. The ravine from which the Indians launched their attack near Becraft's cabin is still a clearly visible landmark. In a conversation with Nancy O'Malley at the University of Kentucky Archeology and Anthropology Department, she indicated that the Morgan's Station site has never been subjected to a professional archeological dig, and is a prime site to be studied. There apparently is a good deal of interest in the Department to conduct a professional survey, but the Department lacks the independent funds with which to pay for the survey.

The Early History of Montgomery County, Kentucky

Montgomery County and The War of Rebellion

[a] Library of the University of North Carolina, "Leeland Hathaway Recollections – Summary" www.lib.unc.edu/mss/inv/h/hathaway,Leeland.html Leeland Hathaway was born on June 4, 1834 at Deer Park Plantation, in Montgomery County, Kentucky. The house was located on the Maysville Pike near what is today the intersection with Interstate 64. He attended Western Military Institute in Georgetown, Kentucky; Kentucky Military Institute in Frankfort, Kentucky; and Transylvania University in Lexington, Kentucky. He was an attorney by profession, and was involved in Kentucky politics. In 1862 he joined John Hunt Morgan's men, serving in the 14th Kentucky Cavalry. He was captured during Morgan's raid into Ohio in 1863, and was held until early 1865. Shortly after his release he found himself in South Carolina and served as an armed escort to Mrs. Jefferson Davis and children as they were making their way toward Florida with the intent of escaping the country with Mr. Davis. He was with Davis' party when they were captured at Irwinville, Georgia on May 10, 1865. He was again imprisoned, and eventually returned to Kentucky to practice law. He died on October 23, 1909 and is buried in the Winchester Cemetery in Winchester, Kentucky.

[b] www.civilwarhome.com/armyeasternkentucky.htm, January 30, 2005. Humphrey Marshall was born in Frankfort, Kentucky on January 13, 1812. He graduated from the United States Military Academy (West Point) in 1832, and a year later resigned his commission to become a lawyer. He fought in the Mexican War and led a charge at Buena Vista. In 1849 he became a member of Congress, and then served as Commissioner to China in 1852. Jefferson Davis appointed him a Brigadier General, and based in part on his recruiting efforts for the Confederacy in Kentucky, he was appointed a small independent command, with the total soldiers varying from 1,500 to about 5,000. His command was known as the Army of Eastern Kentucky, and was charged with conquest of that region. He was driven out of eastern Kentucky by Brigadier General James A. Garfield (who later would become the 20th President of the United States and the second President to be assassinated in office) after the battle of Pound Gap on March 14, 1862. He resigned from the Confederate service in June, 1863 and resumed the practice of law and became a member of the Confederate Congress from Kentucky. He died in Louisville, Kentucky on March 28, 1872.

[c] George Dallas Mosgrove was born in Louisville, Kentucky on August 18, 1844. At age 18 he was living near Carrollton, Kentucky, when during the excitement of Bragg's invasion of Kentucky he enlisted in the Fourth Kentucky Confederate Cavalry on September 10, 1862. He remained a private throughout the war, identifying with men in the ranks

Author's Notes

and observing their feelings; as regimental and then brigade adjutant's clerk he worked at headquarters, came into contact with several of the most colorful commanders of the war, and became an unusually well-informed private. He served under various commanders in eastern Kentucky and Virginia. He was present in Mount Sterling when General Humphrey gave his speech to the new recruits. He published <u>Kentucky Cavaliers in Dixie</u> in 1894. He died on February 21, 1907 near Carrollton.

[d] John Marshall Prewitt relates that Jabez Dooley, the owner of the property, had gone into the Confederate army. His property was seized and used by the Union forces as Camp Dooley.

[e] Roy S. Cluke was born in Clark County, Kentucky and enlisted in the Confederate army. He was commissioned Colonel of the 8th Regiment Kentucky Cavalry in September, 1862 at the height of the Confederate invasion of Kentucky. He rode with John Hunt Morgan in late 1862 through mid-1863. He was captured in late 1863 and died in a Union prison. He is buried near Morgan in the Lexington Cemetery.

[f] According to John Marshall Prewitt, after the war Colonel Stoner lived at "Longwood", the first house on the north side of the Owingsville Road east of I-64. His widow paid for the WWI monument in the Courthouse yard.

[g] Captain Peter M. Everett and his brother, Mack, were residents of Montgomery County. They were strong Confederate sympathizers. The Unionists considered Peter Everett quite notorious, and the secessionists considered him, at the outset of the war, to be quite dashing. By mid-1862 Peter Everett was heavily involved in recruiting for the Confederate army, a dangerous task at the time due to the number of Union soldiers in central Kentucky. On August 6, 1862 the editor of the *Frankfort Tri-Weekly Commonwealth* reported that "three young men, named Frank and Chris Ferguson and Peter Everett are said to be hanging about the town [Mount Sterling] with a force of some fifty to sixty men". Peter Everett was Captain of Company "B", 3rd Battalion, Kentucky Mounted Rifles that was organized in the summer of 1862 with men he recruited from the Maysville area and Montgomery County. His raid on Mount Sterling when he burned the Courthouse in December of 1863 may have tarnished his image with the local sympathizers. Everett's unit served in the Department of East Tennessee, and was involved in skirmishes in Tennessee, Kentucky and Virginia. In the spring of 1865 Captain Everett is said to have been riding in Kentucky with William Clark Quantrill's much reduced force of raiders, dressed in Union uniforms, whose particular vengeance at the time was being extracted from the Negro soldiers fighting in the Union army. The unit surrendered at Bowling Green, Kentucky in April, 1865. It was Mack Everett who, in June 1864, advised General John Hunt Morgan as to the location of the two Union

camps outside of Mount Sterling. (The author continues to search for a photograph of Captain Peter Everett).

[h] According to John Marshall Prewitt, Dr. Benjamin P. Drake lived on the east side of Sycamore Street – then called Factory Street – about halfway between Main Street and High Street – then called Hill Street. The house burned between 1870 and 1875.

[i] The noted chivalry and gallantry of the Confederate soldiers was fading with the failing cause. This was observed by John Marshall Prewitt who noted that there followed a general ransacking of stores and robbing of citizens by the men of the Second Brigade. The First Brigade did not participate, much to First Brigade commander Edward O. Guerrant's satisfaction. "I want our old First Brigade to have no stain of the robber's guilt on its chivalric hands."

[j] In his paper "Montgomery County During the Civil War", John Marshall Prewitt states that Morgan left the First Brigade to wait for the mostly dismounted Third Brigade which apparently arrived by the Camargo Pike and camped somewhere near the present Montgomery County High School. The First Brigade camped on the Owingsville Road, probably near Hinkston Creek in the area of the Fairgrounds. Thus the two brigades were too far apart for mutual support, a tactical error.

[k] John Marshall Prewitt noted that the vault is still installed in the bank's building on the southwest corner of Main and Bank. The present façade of the bank building with the words "Farmer's National Bank" is a later addition. It was not then a National Bank.

Author's Notes

Court Day

[a] In a telephone interview on March 2, 2006 with Judge Cas Lane, he recalled that as a boy growing up in Mount Sterling the third Monday in October (which is the traditional date for the observance of County Court Day) was always the biggest trading day with the most people, and that the second largest trading day was the third Monday in February, when there would be a large volume of mules and horses traded from the upcoming spring planting. He stated that the trading was always done around the Court House and on the lawn of the Court House. With the trading in the center of town, traffic was always tied up in knots and it was a big mess to clean up on the following day. After bitter complaints by the sanitation department, the City Council move the trading along Locust Street and the railroad tracks some time in about 1912. He further recalled that large quantities of coal were purchased for the winter at the October Court Day and delivered to many of the homes in the area. Everything was traded, from sorghum to patent medicine. But the trading was all conducted in one day. It was not until 1971 that the city expanded the current Court Day festival to three days.

[b] In a letter from John Marshall Prewitt dated February 20, 2006, he noted that after the arrival of the railroad to Mount Sterling in 1872 there was soon thereafter a depression that caused all construction to halt for many years. Thus Mount Sterling was "the end of the line". This created great prosperity in the community, as evidenced by the construction dates at the tops of the buildings along Main Street and Maysville Street. Everything that the mountains produced was brought to Mount Sterling to be taken via rail to market. Mr. Prewitt does not believe that there was, in the old days, any official promotion of Court Day. Court Day just grew out of natural economic forces.

Mr. Prewitt also recalls that after Court Day many dogs that were not either sold or traded were simply let loose in the city, and that the police spent a lot of time rounding them up.

Index

Aaron's Run, 5
Adena burial mounds, 3, 7
Adena culture, 3, 6, 16, 34
Adena traits, 7
Alligewi, 1, 8
Allington, Clarinda, 63, 68, 73
Allington, David, 60
Allington, Jacob, 54, 60
Allington, Jonathan, 60
Allington, Old Mrs., 60, 63, 73
Anderson, James, 42, 47
Anderson, Nicholas, 25, 55
Apperson, Richard Jr., 93
Apperson, Richard, Judge, 88
April Court Day, 113
Arthur, William, 56
Baker, Alexander, 60, 68, 73
Baker, John, 54
Baker, Joshua, 68, 70, 75
Baker, Nancy, 73
Baker, Polly, 73
Baker, Susan, 73
Baker, William, 73
Bantas, Abraham, 38
Barnes, Robert, 104
Barnes, White & Co., 102
Beal, Leonard, 26, 28, 126
Beasley's cabin, 25
Becraft, Abraham, 56, 60, 62, 65, 68, 72
Becraft, Benjamin, 72
Becraft, Betsy, 67, 72
Becraft, Rachael, 68, 72
Bedinger, Michael, 49
Berry, Ben, 24
Berry, James, 36, 42, 45, 46, 47
Black Fish, Chief, 2, 49
Black Hoof, 28, 126
Boone, Daniel, 23, 37, 49, 50
Boonesborough, 24, 36, 37, 39, 47, 49, 52, 53
Boyer, Henry, 42, 47
Breastplate, 14
Breckenridge, John C., 77, 83

Brock, Calvin, Judge, 98
Brush Creek, 6, 19, 20
Bryan, Rebecca, 50
Buckner, E.P., 13
Buckner, Simon Bolivar, Gen., 79, 83
Bullitt, Thomas, 2, 51
Burchett mounds, 4
Burchett, D.T., 4
Calk, William, 13, 25, 126, 127
Calloway, John, 37
Calmes, Marquis, Gen., 24, 25, 26, 27
Camargo, Ky, 4, 6, 19
Camp Dooley, 89, 90, 91
Campbell, Rev. John P., 2
Caperton, Adam, 36, 42, 46, 47
Cradlebough, William, 36, 42, 47
Cassidy, Michael, 68, 70
Cattlepool, John, 36
Chartier, Peter, 22, 32, 33, 34
Cherokee traditions, 2, 9
Cherokees, 2
Chisca, 22, 29, 30, 31, 33
Clay, Green, 36, 37
Clay, Henry, 77
Clifton, Daniel, 74
Cluke, Roy S., Col., 90, 91, 92, 93, 94, 95, 96, 97, 99, 133
Cockrell, Clell, 15
Cockrell, George B., 15
Cofer, Rueben, 56, 72
Colefoot, John, 36, 42, 45, 47
Combs, Benjamin, Capt., 24, 25
Combs, Cuthbert, 24, 25, 26
Combs, Joseph, 24
Congleton's Hill, 91
Connelly, Arthur, 58
Cook, David, Ens., 36, 42, 45, 47
Cornstalk, Chief, 125
Craig, Robert, 56, 60, 63, 67, 72
Crawford, John, 58, 75
Crim, William, 42, 47

Index

Crittenden, John J., 77, 81
Crockett, Martha, 55
Curtright, Peter, 56, 60
Daniels, Major, 27, 28
Delawares, 2, 32, 39
Deron, Daniel, 56, 61
Dooley, Jabez, 133
Dougherty, Robert, 51
Douglas, David, 73
Douglas, James, 51, 53
Douglas, John, 50
Douglas, Mary, 50
Downing, Samuel, 74
Dr. Hannah's Orchard, 96
Drake & Bosworth's Woolen Mill, 95
Drake, Dr. Benjamin P., 94, 101, 134
Duncan, Andrew, 56, 60, 61, 62, 73
Easton, Thomas, 27
Epperson, Richard, 37
Eskippakithiki, 22, 23, 24, 30, 31, 32, 33, 34, 126
Estill, James, Capt., 36, 37, 38, 42, 44, 46, 47
Estill, Monk – See Monk
Estill, Samuel, 36, 38
Estill's Spring, 41
Estill's Station, 36, 38, 39, 40, 41, 47
Ethnology, Bureau of, 10
Evans, John, Capt., 84
Everett, Mack, 100
Everett, Peter M., Capt., 86, 92, 98, 100, 133, 134
Farmer's Bank of Kentucky, 102
February Court Day, 113
Ferguson, Frank, 98
Findley, John, 23, 24
Forbes, ____, 42, 44, 47
Forbes, Hugh, 57, 58
Fort, Peter, 55, 65
Fowler, Moses, 69, 70, 71
Frazer, David, 25, 26
Funkhouser, W.D., 12, 15
Gaitskill mound, 3, 7, 17, 18, 19

Gaitskill tablets, 17, 18, 19
Gass, David, Capt., 36, 40
Gass, Jennie, 40, 42
Gass, John, 40
Gay, Weed, 90
George, Whitson, 42, 47
Giants, 9, 10, 11, 12
Goff, Elisha, 126
Goode, R.R., Surgeon, 102
Gough, Thomas Mrs., 26, 27, 28
Grassy Lick Creek, 5, 6
Grassy Lick, 28, 61
Greenbriar Branch, 5, 6
Greenway, G., 19
Greer, Walker, 4
Hackett, Peter, 36, 40, 41, 42, 47
Hancock, Stephen, 37
Hanks, John, 75
Hanks, Peter, 51, 53
Hanks, William, 51, 53
Hansford, Rev., 61
Hansford, Thomas, 60
Harper, George, 75
Harper, John, 25, 53, 127
Harper, Peter, 53
Harper's Creek, 5, 51, 54, 60
Harper's Ridge, 51
Hart, Josiah (Si), 51
Hasty, John, 54
Hathaway, Leeland, 80, 132
Hazelrigg, Dillard, 105
Heckwelder, John, 9
Highland, J.P., 5
Hinkston Creek, 5, 13, 42, 43, 55, 57
Hoffman, William, 102
Holder, John, Capt., 49
Home Guard, 78, 80, 82, 83, 84, 88, 89, 93, 99
Hood, John Bell, Gen., 75, 105
Hood, Luke, 75
Hopewell culture, 3
Howard's Creek, 22, 24, 26, 27, 29
Howe, W.T., 95
Indian Fort, 6, 19, 34

Iroquois, 1, 2, 32, 39
Irvine, John, 56
Irvine, William, Col., 42, 43, 46, 47
James, Ward, Capt., 59, 69, 70, 71, 72
Jameson, John, 42, 47
Jeffersonville, Ky, 88, 93, 98
Jesse, George M., Capt., 83
Jesuit Relations, 31
Johnson, _____, 42, 45, 47
Johnson, Jacob, 6
Jones, Joseph, 69, 71
Judy, John, 39, 57
Judy, R.T., 4
Kelly, Beal, 42, 47
Kenton, Simon, 65, 68, 70, 71
Knox, Raymond, 5
Kratzer, Lawrence, 5
Lane, James, 73, 74, 75, 131
Lenni-Lenapi, 1
Little Mountain, 3, 13, 41, 42, 52, 57, 58
Lockhart, Levi, 75
Logan, Benjamin, Capt., 39
Lulbegrud Creek, 5, 22, 23, 24, 26, 33, 55
Lusby's Mill, 81
Lyle, Clark, 93
Lynch, David, 36, 42, 47
Machpelah Cemetary, 105
Maginty, Alexander, 126
Magistrates, 108, 109
Magoffin, Beriah, 78, 79, 80
Marchant, 26
Marshall, Humphrey, Gen., 81, 82, 86, 88, 94, 132
Martin, Elizabeth, 73
Martin, Harry, 54, 56, 60, 61, 63, 72, 75
Martin, John, 72
Martin, Sarah, 72
Massey, Nathaniel, 68, 70
McClellan, George, 78, 79, 80, 81
McCullough, John, 76
McCullough, William, 76

McGee's Station, 47, 52
McKee, Samuel, Capt., 88, 89, 95, 97
McKee, W.R., Mayor, 15
McMillan, Jonathan, 42, 43, 47
McNeally, Michael, 42, 45, 47
Midland Trail, 5
Miller, James, 36
Miller, Thomas, 36
Miller, William, Lt., 42, 44, 45, 47, 129
Miller's Station, 39
Monk, 40, 41, 42, 43, 45, 47
Montgomery, Tom, 51, 55
Mooney, James, 8
Moore, Col. James, 2
Moore, Robert, 57
Morgan, Abel, 73
Morgan, Drusilla, 76
Morgan, John Hunt, Gen., 83, 86, 88, 100, 102
Morgan, Ralph, 49, 50, 51, 54, 56, 75
Morgan, Sarah, 72, 76
Mosgrove, George Dallas, 89, 100, 101, 103, 104, 106, 132
Mount Sterling, Ky., 3, 12, 13, 39, 52, 54, 58, 73, 82, 83, 84, 86, 89, 94, 95, 98, 100, 101, 112, 113, 114
Muddy Creek, 36, 37, 38, 46
Mulberry Lick, 38
Myers, Jacob, 49, 50
Naylor, George, 51
October Court Day, 112, 115
Oil Springs, 27, 32
Orear, Lee, 104
Parsons, Thomas, W., 82, 85, 89, 91, 95, 97, 99, 102
Peeled Oak, 56, 60, 63
Pilot's Knob, 23
Pleake, John, 56, 60, 61
Pound Gap Road, 82, 83, 99, 100, 105, 112
Powell, John Wesley, 10
Powhatan Confederacy, 2
Prewitt Station, 5

Index

Prewitt, Allen J., 6
Prewitt, Clifton, 85
Prewitt, John Magarvey, Dr.,80
Prewitt, John Marshall, 85
Proctor, Joseph, 36, 42, 45, 46, 47
Proctor, Nicholas, 36
Proctor, Rueben, 42, 47, 56
Rafinesque, C.S. Prof., 19
Ratliff, William D., Capt., 94, 95, 96, 97
Reed, Spencer, 127
Reppert, Sallie, 84
Rickets, T.J., 93
Ricketts Mound, 3, 7, 15, 16, 17
Riddle, Steven – See Ruddell, Steven
Risk, William, 26
Robertson, Alexander, 40
Robertson, George, Chief Justice, 36
Robinson, George, 36
Rogers, Joseph, 36, 42, 47
Round Head, 43
Ruddell, Steven, 28, 125
Sand Island, 2
Sco-tach, Chief, 71
Shane, John D, Rev., 25, 26, 27, 74, 75
Sherley, Mike, 36
Simpson, Joe, 58
Skaggs, Solomon, 56
Slate Creek, 6, 50, 56, 59, 63
Smith, Enoch, 13, 25, 26, 53, 54, 57, 58, 66, 68, 73
Smith, John, Lt., 36
Snow, Charles E., 7
Soto, Hernando de, 9, 22, 30
South, John Jr., Lt., 42, 45, 47
South, John, 43
South, Samuel, 40, 41, 42
Spencer Creek, 6
Split Log, 43, 129
Spratt Mound, 3
Spratt, Dr. S. E., 3
Stafford, B, 4
Stand-In-Water, 59, 69, 71

Stepstone Creek, 6, 55, 65
Stoner, Robert G., Lt. Col., 91, 92, 94, 133
Storkes, Jeremiah, 25
Strode, John, 49, 50
Strode's Station, 39, 47, 50, 53, 53, 58
Sudduth, William, 52, 57, 74
Sutawnee, 58, 59, 69, 70, 71
Sutton, William, 113
Swearingen, Andrew, 75
Swearingen, Benoni, 49
Swearingen, Thomas, 49
Thomas, Cyrus, 10
Thompson, John A., 91
Tipton, William, 91
Troutman, John, 56
Troutman, Peter, 73
Vallandingham's Barn, 81
Voris, William, 84
Wade, Dawson, 60
Wade, James, 51, 53, 54, 56, 57, 60, 61, 64, 66, 72, 74, 75
Wade, John, 52, 53, 54, 56, 57
Wafford, James, 8, 9
Walker, Robert, 57
Wallam Olum, 1
Ward, James, Capt., 69, 70, 72
Ward, John, 59, 69
Warren, Thomas, 36
Warren, William, 54
Warrior's Path (Trace) 12, 22, 23, 29, 30, 32, 36
Webb, William S., 7, 12, 15, 17
White Wolf, 58, 59, 61, 65, 69, 71
Whitledg, Robert, 25
Whitley, William, 73
Wills, John, 90
Wright-Green mounds, 7, 17
Young, Bennett H., 92
Young, Elizabeth, 73
Young, Joseph, 60, 62, 63, 68, 72
Young, Nat, 4

www.ingramcontent.com/pod-product-compliance
Lightning Source LLC
Chambersburg PA
CBHW051931160426
43198CB00012B/2115